—LIVING ON THE—
EDGE OF
HEAVEN

Chad Daybell

—Living on the—
Edge of Heaven

by Chad Daybell

spring creek
BOOK COMPANY
Rexburg, Idaho

ISBN 13: 978-1-944657-01-7

e. 1

Published by:
Spring Creek Book Company
P.O. Box 1013
Rexburg, Idaho 83440

www.springcreekbooks.com

Cover design © Spring Creek Book Company

Printed in the United States of America
Printed on acid-free paper

DEDICATION

To Tammy,
my one and only.

She doesn't like the limelight,
but deserves all of the credit.

Table of Contents

AUTHOR'S NOTE

This book is not my full autobiography. I mainly hit the highlights of how the Lord has guided me through certain situations, and how my interactions with the Spirit World have impacted my decisions.

I discuss why I write my novels and publish books by other people who have had near-death experiences.

When I have used a person's full name, I have either received his or her permission, or I feel the story is generic enough that it won't harm the person's reputation.

In regard to my missionary companions, I only used their last names. In other cases I have simply used first names, or changed the name to protect the person's privacy.

There are dozens of friends, relatives, and authors who have made a powerful impact on me that aren't mentioned in these pages, simply because of the unique nature of the book. Please know I greatly appreciate each of you, and I hope you enjoy this glimpse into an aspect of my life that I kept hidden for many years.

INTRODUCTION

The idea for this book actually came after a discussion with my father. He was preparing to teach a lesson to his High Priests group, and he was looking for any instances that spoke of "familial councils" on the other side of the veil. He had been taught privately by Church leaders about this principle, but such a concept is virtually absent in the current curriculum.

As a Church we talk about family history a lot, focusing on the souls trapped in Spirit Prison who need us to do their temple work. But we rarely mention our righteous ancestors who are closely watching us from the other side of the veil.

In this book you'll read of several instances where I have been able to receive their guidance. I believe that just as we hold family councils on this side of the veil, similar meetings are being held there, too, with the focus on how to help those of us on earth. That perspective can help us unify our families and bring a broader view of our missions in life.

When the angel Moroni visited young Joseph Smith in his bedroom in 1827, he quoted Malachi a little differently than is found in the Bible: *And **he shall plant** in the hearts of the children **the promises made** to the fathers, and the hearts of the children **shall turn** to their fathers. If it were not so, the whole earth would be utterly wasted at his coming. (Joseph Smith History 1:39)*

I believe we made agreements with our close relatives before we came to earth. We are now seeking to fulfill those promises, and our relatives who have passed on are also striving to keep the promises they made to us. It's a glorious concept as we work together from both sides of the veil.

Another purpose of this book is to provide assurance and comfort to those who have also felt "on the edge of heaven."

You are not alone. Over the past few years as my life story has become more well-known, I have received hundreds of emails from people who were happy to find someone who has had similar experiences.

I understand how they feel. After all, I have waited several years to share the unusual experiences contained in this book. Why? Because I feared that my family and friends might think I had gone crazy.

This reluctance within the LDS Church to share spiritual experiences is a rather recent phenomenon. After all, the Church itself was established and fortified through miraculous visitations from heavenly messengers.

For the first 160 years after the Church was established by Joseph Smith in 1830, sharing inspiring spiritual experiences was quite common. Lengthy near-death experiences and accounts of visitations from deceased ancestors were regularly printed in the *Deseret News* and other Church publications through the 1930s. Many books were compiled of these experiences, and I have them in my personal library.

For the past few years, though, there has been a subtle trend to discourage the sharing of personal spiritual experiences. I don't believe this is what the Lord intended. He makes it clear in the scriptures that we should edify each other through inspiring words, rather than cast stones at those who seek to share uplifting messages.

Some members take an excerpt from a 1971 talk by Elder Boyd K. Packer and say we shouldn't discuss special experiences. However, it is important to read the quote in context:

Occasionally during the past year I have been asked a question. Usually it comes as a curious, almost an idle, question about the qualifications to stand as a witness for Christ. The question they ask is, "Have you seen Him?"

That is a question that I have never asked of another. I have not asked that question of my brethren in the Quorum, thinking that it would be so sacred and so personal that one would have to have some special inspiration, indeed, some authorization, even to ask it.

There are some things just too sacred to discuss. We know that as it relates to the temples. In our temples, sacred ordinances are performed; sacred experiences are enjoyed. And yet we do not, because of the nature of them, discuss them outside those sacred walls.

It is not that they are secret, but they are sacred; not to be discussed, but to be harbored and to be protected and regarded with the deepest of reverence.

President Packer was talking about the actual appearance of Jesus Christ to a mortal. He also mentioned the sacredness of the temple ordinances. I agree completely with President Packer that those items fall in the "too sacred to discuss" category!

I've had many sacred moments in my life that will never be shared publicly. I guard them and treat them with reverence, and they aren't included in this book.

However, many of my experiences are simply out of the ordinary or unusual, rather than sacred. We sometimes forget that we are spiritual beings having a physical experience. This earth is a tiny portion of a grand cosmic operation. Our "real life" isn't on this planet.

We are part of an eternal family, and it only makes sense we would feel a connection to our ancestors on the other side of the veil. They are fully aware of what we are doing, and they seek to help us when we need it.

Nearly every culture on earth feels this way about their ancestors except the Western world. We have let our "spirituality pendulum" swing to a low point in the past few years where we only believe in things that can be verified by our five senses.

Hopefully the pendulum is starting to swing back so that we can share sincere, humble spiritual experiences again. Recent talks in General Conference by several General Authorities, including apostles Elder Henry B. Eyring and Elder Russell M. Nelson, shared personal stories involving the Spirit World, and a re-awakening seems to be happening within the Church.

We can still read and cherish the amazing experiences the early Saints had, but it is time for living, breathing LDS members to add their stories to this collection. I'm not saying all of these experiences need to be published—or even posted on Facebook—but if you've had such an experience, please record it for your posterity.

I hope this book demonstrates that "visionary" people can live normal lives, be fully active in the Church, and wholeheartedly sustain the General Authorities.

The visionaries I have met are humble followers of the Lord, and I expect the number of dreams and visions to increase among the Saints as times get tougher and we rely more on personal revelation to guide us.

Well, on with the story. I've had an unusual life, and I'm grateful for the chance to share these experiences with you!

Chad Daybell
May 2017

CHAPTER ONE

Leaping Into Eternity

On a sunny day in August 1985, I stood on the edge of a 60-foot-high cliff overlooking Flaming Gorge Reservoir in northern Utah. I felt dizzy just looking down at the water, but I knew I needed to jump to impress the other young men from my LDS Church group.

We had started the day by leaping off cliffs that were about 20-feet high. That was fun, but we noticed this particular cliff jutting out over the water. It looked like a natural diving board. My friends and I watched someone else jump from the ledge, and soon we were scrambling up the hillside.

Once we got up there and saw how high it truly was, we were intimidated, but we were also stupid teenagers. My pals finally convinced me to go first.

I had just turned 17 and was heading into my senior year at Springville High School, where I would serve on the Student Council. I had a summer job with the Springville City Parks Department as a maintenance worker, but other than that, life was pretty carefree.

I had experienced some close calls the previous few months, though. I had recently gone on a water-skiing trip to Lake Powell, and while being pulled by the boat, I fell face-first into the water.

The tip of one of the skis smacked me in the face and briefly knocked me out. I suffered a deep gash between my nose and upper lip that took 12 stitches to close. I still have that scar, and it has made it impossible for me to ever grow a decent mustache.

A few weeks after that, I had gone golfing with my friends. On one hole I hit my tee shot then stood against a tree about thirty yards up the fairway as the final member of our foursome took his turn. He took a mighty swing and drilled the ball right at me! I barely had time to duck. The ball grazed the top of my head, then made a small indention in the tree before dropping to the ground behind me.

My friend hurried toward me and shouted, "Whoa! I thought I killed you!"

There were similar incidents that summer, and I felt somewhat like a marked man. I sensed that someone didn't necessarily want me dead, but only "mostly dead," to steal a line from *The Princess Bride*. Jumping off this cliff wasn't helping my odds.

I shook off my nervousness and took another long look at the blue water below me. Finally I pushed off with my right foot and began my descent. I remember thinking, "This is taking a really long time."

When I finally hit the water, it felt like I had slammed into concrete. A shock went through my entire body and I saw a white flash of light. I felt an audible pop at the base of my skull, and I thought, "Oh no, I broke my neck." I also wondered if I had cut my forehead open, because there was a brief searing pain above my eyes.

I quickly realized something even worse was happening— my spirit was partly out of my body!

The best way to describe it is my physical body went deeper into the water than my spirit did. This caused my spirit to pop out through my head, but then it felt like my spirit's knees got stuck in my skull and I didn't make it all the way out.

This photo shows the approximate height of the cliff I jumped off that caused my first near-death experience. What a dumb decision!

During those few moments I could see on the other side of the veil I saw an endless white plain in all directions. There seemed to be a distinct horizon hundreds of miles in the distance. I also heard a deep, rich melody that sounded like a synthesizer. The pain I felt a few moments earlier was gone. There was a soothing warmth surrounding me, and I also felt tangible energy particles of knowledge rushing toward me from all directions. I just soaked it all in.

Within seconds, though, my body started to float toward the surface. My spirit quickly reversed course through my head and got sucked back into place. I instantly felt chilled and somewhat paralyzed.

I must have taken a long time getting to the surface, because one of my friends who was standing on the shore had jumped into the water to rescue me. He grabbed hold of me, and we swam to the water's edge. All I said was, "Something snapped when I hit the surface. I'm done for the day."

A Change of Perspective

My entire body was sore for a week, and even then I felt off-kilter, like my body and spirit were disjointed. Sometimes my right eye would just go blind, but if I hit the side of my head with my palm, I could see again. I didn't tell my parents about it. I was an invincible teenager, right? Why bother?

On the other hand, I was spiritually changed. I had glimpsed another dimension, and it had felt like home.

I didn't recall talking to anyone in the white light, but I remembered the infusion of spiritual energy that had surrounded me. I now had an interest in gospel topics like never before and began to devour Church-related books—the scriptures, Cleon Skousen, Hugh Nibley, Bruce R. McConkie, and so on.

I had the strong impression I would need this information

later in life. I still had a social life and a great set of friends, but I became very receptive to sensing disembodied spirits, as well as receiving direct promptings and impressions that helped keep me out of danger.

This change was quite a letdown when it came to dating. If I dated a girl I really liked more than two or three times, the Spirit didn't mess around when I prayed whether the relationship should develop. Almost before the words were out of my mouth, I would hear a resounding "NO!"

That was disheartening in the short term, but I hoped it meant there was someone very special out there who would become my better half.

In retrospect, I believe when I hit the water and my spirit exited my body, my personal "veil" was torn open near my forehead and never sealed back up properly. That's why I felt physically out of sync.

As I think back on the other previous "accidents" that summer, I believe that they were attempts to accomplish what had happened at Flaming Gorge. To fulfill my mission in life, I needed a good shot to the head to tear my veil a little, and the angels finally orchestrated it!

CHAPTER TWO

※

Faithful Forefathers

In order for you to fully appreciate the rest of the story, I need to share a few important tidbits about my ancestry.

If you are acquainted with any of my Daybell relatives, I hope you consider them to be good-hearted, hard-working people. We rarely serve higher in the Church beyond being a bishop or a Relief Society president, and a lot of us would much rather be at the rodeo or in the mountains than at our Sunday meetings. But when the going gets tough, you can be sure we'll be there to help in any way we can.

Nearly all of the Daybells in the western United States come from the same common ancestor, Finity Daybell. He and his wife Mary joined the LDS Church in England during the 1840s, but they were too poor to travel to the United States during the mass Mormon migration in the 1850s.

Finity had strained his back hauling lumber, and the family spent time living in an actual poorhouse when he couldn't work. By the early 1860s, Finity's health was restored and the family was doing better financially.

At that time, Elder Joseph F. Smith, a future president of the Church, was serving a mission in England. The missionaries faced a lot of persecution and even death threats, yet they continued preaching the gospel.

One day Elder Smith and his companion were speaking to a crowd in the town square. Soon a man in the crowd brought out a basket of rotten eggs, and he and his friends began throwing the eggs at the missionaries. Elder Smith was wearing a stovepipe hat, and an egg splattered against it.

At this moment, Finity came into the square. He had come to town to fix his plow, but when he saw what was happening to Elder Smith, he took action. He knew the missionaries had been told not to fight back against their persecutors, but he knew that he certainly could!

Finity ran toward the men who were throwing the eggs. He grabbed the egg basket from the ringleader and swung it forcefully at the man's head. He didn't hit anyone with his swing, but the men knew he meant business and quickly scattered as Finity reared back and swung again.

Soon only Finity and the two missionaries stood in the square. Elder Smith stepped forward and thanked Finity for his courage.

Moving to Utah

That experience helped Finity realize he needed to move his family to Utah. They saved up their money for two years, and then made the trek in May 1864. They traveled by ship to New York Harbor in the midst of the U.S. Civil War. Finity found a spot for his family in a train boxcar heading west, but their journey was often delayed because the train tracks had been uprooted by the warring armies. They finally left the train behind and took a steamboat to Nebraska, then made the rest of journey to Utah in wagons. They finally reached Salt Lake City in October, five grueling months after they had departed from England.

Finity Daybell brought his family from England to Utah in 1864 and helped settle the town of Charleston in the Heber Valley.

Finity sought out Elder Joseph E. Taylor, who had baptized him many years earlier. Joseph said he had some property near the town of Heber, and Finity offered to farm it. The family traveled to the area at the top of Provo Canyon now known as Charleston. They barely survived a horrible winter living in muddy dugouts in the side of a hill, but the next spring Finity and his sons established their farm and became prominent citizens there.

I'm the descendant of Finity's son George, who became a

well-known landowner and farmer. However, on a clear summer day in 1913, George's life was cut short when a bolt of lightning struck him as he raised a pitchfork into the air while moving hay. He was killed instantly.

George's son Robert took over the farm, but in 1925, the family learned the soon-to-be-built Deer Creek Reservoir would eventually cover their property with water.

Robert scraped together the money he had and made a payment on a house in the Provo river bottoms. The home was smaller than they were accustomed to, but it had five acres of land, including an apple orchard. Robert went to work using a set of draft horses to dig basements and plow garden spots. He also earned money harvesting fruit.

In the summer of 1929 the family moved to a nicer home on south State Street in Provo. Robert and his brother Will went into business raising chickens. They built large coops and bought dozens of baby chicks, building up a substantial debt.

Later that year their worst nightmares came true. The stock market crash in October 1929 ruined the economy. The brothers lost everything they owned, including the house, and suddenly the family was in the depths of poverty.

Robert was able to rent a house in southwest Provo, and the family lived there throughout the Great Depression. Robert was able to find work through government programs, but it was hardly enough to support the family.

Horsing Around

Robert had a son named Keith, who become my grandpa. Keith was 10 years old when the Great Depression hit, and his mother kept him busy doing chores and small jobs to help the family stay afloat.

Keith's parents rarely had reason to be angry with him, except for one little adventure while he was attending Dixon Junior High in Provo. He'd been riding his horse near the school when he noticed some girls on the playground. He started chasing the girls around, making them scream. They started running into the school, with Keith right behind them on the horse. They headed up the school steps and flung open the doors. Before the doors could close, Keith made it into the school—horse and all! This caused quite a scene, and both the school teachers and his parents were mighty upset with him.

Keith loved horses, but he may have had second thoughts the day he tried to shoe one of them. As he bent down to grab the horse's leg, he got kicked squarely in the mouth, cracking one of his front teeth. A dentist placed a gold cap on the tooth, and from then on Keith was a bit more careful around horses' hooves.

Keith had met Rosalie Bjarnson the previous spring at Springville High's Junior Prom. Rather than taking dates during those lean years, students would go in groups then mingle at the dance. Keith and his friends had decided to drive over from Provo and drop in on the dance.

Keith and Rosalie got to know each other, but Keith's other two friends actually asked Rosalie out first. She said the first friend turned out to be "obnoxious," and the second friend also failed to catch her fancy. So Keith finally asked her out, and they had a pleasant time.

Rosalie found herself attracted to Keith's kind, happy personality, and his blue eyes. He combed his brown hair straight back, but she liked it when it would get ruffled and curl a bit on the sides. They were soon going steady.

They spent Easter hiking up Springville's Round Peak for lunch, and they took a horseback ride up Provo's Rock Canyon that summer, which was Rosalie's first time on a horse. They dated for more than a year before being married in 1937.

The couple had planned on being married in an LDS temple, and Rosalie was able to receive a temple recommend, but due to Keith's work schedule, he had been unable to attend church very often. Keith enjoyed church, but found himself scheduled to work most Sundays. His bishop felt Keith should wait before receiving a recommend, so the marriage was performed at Rosalie's parents' home in Springville.

As the wedding was about to start, all the invited guests were there—except Keith. Rosalie began to wonder if she'd been stood up. Keith finally rushed in a few minutes later, explaining the gold cap on his front tooth had fallen off, and he had hurried to the dentist for a little cement to keep it in place.

It was tradition for friends of a newly married couple to try to keep them apart for as long as possible after the ceremony and make them suffer through embarrassing pranks. This mischief could last for at least a day or two, and Keith and Rosalie wanted to avoid being separated on their wedding night.

Rosalie had heard that her friends had borrowed a large baby buggy with plans of putting a bonnet on her head and parading her down Provo's Center Street. Keith's friends had similar plans for him, so the couple enlisted the help of his sister Eva and her husband Paul.

After the ceremony, the newlyweds rushed to the garage, hopped into Paul and Eva's car and sped away. They had arranged to stay at Paul and Eva's house for the night, while Paul and Eva took Keith's car and spent the night at a motel. The plan worked just fine, foiling the friends' pranks.

War Overshadows Daily Life

Keith and Rosalie had a simple but happy life together, and they welcomed the birth of their son Ray in 1939.

However, on December 7, 1941, Japan launched a surprise

attack on Hawaii's Pearl Harbor, drawing the United States into World War II. Young American men were drafted into the Armed Forces and trained for battle.

The government first drafted single men in their late teens, but as the war dragged on and the casualties mounted, older men and even married men were drafted to serve their country. Keith was willing to serve his country, but he felt anxious about possibly being drafted and leaving his young family, especially since the war didn't appear anywhere near a conclusion.

Keith opened a Texaco gas station on the northeast corner of 400 North and Main Street in Springville, where a doctor's clinic is now located. Ray had grown to be a healthy, fun-loving and slightly mischievous child, and in early 1944 he gained a brother with similar qualities named Lanny.

Rosalie's brothers Leon, Glenn and Hosmer were all enlisted in the armed services by then. Then in May a dreaded letter arrived— Keith had been drafted into the infantry, and he would likely be on the battlefront in Europe by the end of the year. This was a heavy burden for both Keith and Rosalie. Although many other families faced similar situations, it still didn't ease the ache in their hearts.

Keith departed for Camp Roberts in California for four months of heavy training before entering active duty. Keith and Rosalie wrote to each other every night and sent photographs. He was assigned to a platoon known as "The Railsplitters," and he grew close to his fellow soldiers. In October 1944 they flew to Europe and began to work their way toward the front lines. He found time to write home a letter, saying he was "somewhere in Holland," and that he was fine and that the family shouldn't worry.

The platoon soon reached the battle zone, and they encountered fierce fighting. Keith was forced to take the lives of opposing soldiers or be killed himself by the enemy. In one instance, a German sniper was hiding in a tree. He was slowly but surely killing several of the American soldiers. Keith took it upon himself to end the threat, and he shot the sniper from the tree. The man fell to the ground, and as Keith rolled him over, he saw a blond young man no older than 16 who looked similar to his own brothers-in-law. It sickened him, but the experience possibly helped prepare him for the trials that lay ahead.

He got along well with his fellow soldiers and was nicknamed "The Utah Kid." On Thanksgiving Day 1944 he wrote to say he was in his foxhole eating turkey out of a tin can, and that despite the snowy, cold conditions, the meal tasted quite good.

His platoon moved forward, and December began with Keith becoming the platoon leader, due to his own leader being killed. Sometime during the fighting, a shell hit a wall close to Keith. The impact sent fragments of the wall flying toward him, and one piece cracked his knee cap. It slowly healed, but it would occasionally give him trouble throughout the rest of his life.

Keith's platoon chiseled foxholes out of the frozen soil, awaiting a German attack. On December 3rd, the attack came. Soon only seven platoon members were still alive. The German tanks rumbled toward the soldiers, with the tank drivers spinning their tracks, trying to crush the soldiers in the foxholes. Keith and his fellow soldiers ran from their foxholes to a large shell hole, hoping it would provide more protection. Then all they could do was lie low and hope to go undetected.

One German tank rumbled past them, and they gave sighs of relief as it continued on. Then suddenly the tank stopped, shifted gears and reversed to a stop right over the hole. The men were sure they would be killed. The tank began to grind its tracks, but the soldiers were able to avoid death. After a minute, a door in the belly of the tank opened up, and the Americans were pulled into the tank as prisoners of war.

My grandpa Keith Daybell at Camp Roberts in California before heading to the front lines in Europe.

A Prisoner of War

Keith was taken to a prison camp known as "Stalag II" near Frankfurt, Germany. The prisoners were placed in a wire enclosure without much protection from the elements. However, they did receive Red Cross packages, which contained cigarettes. Keith didn't smoke, and he would trade his cigarettes to an older woman who would come to the fence offering "black bread." Keith and his fellow soldiers would also mix their sugar ration in with snow to make their own version of ice cream.

Before Keith had left Springville, he had arranged for a bouquet of red roses to be delivered to Rosalie on Christmas Day. It was a welcome surprise to see the attached card in Keith's handwriting, written months earlier. However, the joy was diminished the next day when Rosalie received a notice that Keith was listed as "missing in action." The postmaster had received the message on Christmas Day, but he decided to wait a day to deliver it, rather than spoil the holiday for the family.

Some family members feared Keith was dead, but his father Robert encouraged the family to never give up hope that his son was still alive.

At about that time, Keith and his fellow prisoners were told they were being transferred to a bigger barracks. The rough winter had already taken a toll on the prisoners, and the long march to the barracks added to their physical troubles. Keith's feet had become frozen, and although he struggled to keep up with the group, he finally couldn't walk any further. Other soldiers tried to help him along, but the effort was slowing down the group. A German guard ordered the men to leave Keith along the side of the road and let him die. However, fellow prisoner George Wells Hurt, known as "Tex" to his fellow soldiers, refused the order. He found a wooden plank and told Keith to rest on the board, with his arms and legs dangling. Tex and another prisoner then carried Keith the rest of the way to the barracks. Once they arrived there, Tex rubbed Keith's feet with snow until feeling began to return, helping save his feet from permanent damage. Keith was always grateful to Tex for not only saving his feet, but also his life.

By early 1945, the Allied forces were making great strides against their Axis foes. American bombers were flying far into German territory, making successful attacks on key cities and railroads. The Germans relied heavily on their railroads, and so they would send American prisoners out to repair damaged rails rather than risk the lives of their own people.

Keith found himself patching together German railroads, facing the risk of being accidentally killed by his own country's bombers. It was difficult work, and combined with the poor food and rough living conditions, the prisoners began to lose weight and strength. Yet they faced death at the hands of the German guards if they didn't work, so they pushed on.

The prisoners were transported to the work sites in train boxcars. The Germans would force several dozen prisoners into each boxcar, leaving little room to do much more than stand. Most of the soldiers were so weak that once the train began to move they would slump down and try to sleep, lying on their sides on the hard wooden boxcar floor. There wasn't room to lie flat, and as the train moved along, the bumps and jostles would injure and irritate the soldiers' shoulders and hips. Keith would always have trouble sleeping on his right side because of those boxcar injuries.

One night the prisoners were being held in a building and forced to sleep on a concrete floor. Suddenly the German guards stormed in. They said a train had passed by and a fire had started in the weeds. They blamed the Americans and said someone needed to pay for what had happened. A guard rushed forward, pointed his gun at the prisoner lying next to Keith, and shot him to death. Keith later told Rosalie it was simply luck that it hadn't been him.

The prisoners would sometimes find dead, rotting horses and other animals as they worked along the tracks. They gladly ate the animals, cooking the meat when possible. They considered this a step up from their prison meals, which were so meager the prisoners' cooks would mix sawdust into the bread dough just to make the ingredients last a little longer.

In August 1945, Russian troops advanced toward Keith's barracks and released the prisoners. The Russians loaded them into trucks and took them to freedom. The worries weren't over for the Americans, however, as the celebrating Russian soldiers drank bottle after bottle of vodka. The joyful-but-drunk drivers somehow kept the trucks from going off the narrow, mountainous roads.

Keith was released from prison weighing 95 pounds, down from the already lean 170 pounds he weighed before the war. After so many months as a prisoner, his hair had grown down past his shoulders and he had a full beard.

He was sent to an Army hospital in Europe, where he put on weight fairly quickly. He was then transferred to a hospital in San Diego for two weeks. He resumed his Army duties there, where he was given the responsibility of guarding Italian prisoners. Rosalie and the boys went there to stay with him during this time. He was released from the Army on Thanksgiving Day 1945 and attended a banquet where he was served a big turkey dinner, which brought back memories of 1944's foxhole turkey dinner.

Keith was awarded two Purple Hearts by the U.S. government for wounds he suffered in battle, along with other honors for his acts of heroism during the war.

Returning to Civilian Life

When he returned to Springville, Keith adjusted quite easily back to civilian life. Keith joined his brothers Theo and LaVar in their new Daybell Lumber Company. They formed a logging camp at Soapstone Basin in the Uinta Mountains, and they would cut and haul pine logs from as far south as Scofield before bringing the lumber to Springville to process it. Keith shouldered the responsibility of running the Uinta camp and trucking the lumber down the canyon.

In the fall of 1946, Keith took his father Robert and Rosalie's brothers deer hunting up Hall's Fork in Hobble Creek Canyon. As they were hunting, a man in another hunting party shot at what he thought was a deer, but instead he hit Robert in the thigh. Robert cried out, "I'm hit! I'm hit!" The man came closer to look, but once he saw what he had done, he and his young son headed down the mountain without helping.

Keith and the others finally found Robert, and they laid him over the back of a horse. The wound was just below the hip and despite the use of a tourniquet, it was bleeding heavily.

They reached a man's jeep, put Robert in the back seat and rushed him to the hospital. He had lost nearly two pints of blood, but thankfully Keith, Theo and LaVar all had the correct blood type to donate blood to their father. Robert's life was saved, but his leg had to be amputated. Robert never let the incident get him down, though, and he got along fine with a plastic prosthetic leg and a cane.

My father Jack joined Keith and Rosalie's family in 1947, and the older boys welcomed home their baby brother. Over the next few years, the lumber business thrived, and Keith began plans to build a larger home for his growing family. A baby girl named Judy was born in early 1951.

Above: Rosalie and Keith with Lanny and Ray soon after his return from World War II.

Right: After his return from World War II, Keith made the most of life, including hunting and fishing often to provide food for his family. He appears to have caught his limit of trout this day!

An Unthinkable Tragedy Strikes

Keith began August 9, 1951, at home in Springville, awakening from what he called "the best night's sleep I have ever had." He had traveled to Springville the previous afternoon. He and another man had each shot a deer that day at the lumber mill, and when one of his employees began to feel ill, Keith offered to take him home, since he now had a deer he wanted to drop off to Rosalie anyway.

Keith headed back up to Soapstone Basin, arriving as his employees prepared to lift a large diesel engine off the back of an Army flatbed truck with a smaller A-frame truck.

Before Keith arrived that day, the smaller truck had actually tipped over on the first try and had torn apart the drive line. The men had repaired the truck and were preparing for another attempt when Keith reached camp.

As they continued the project, Keith chatted happily with the men, telling them how Rosalie had dressed Judy in a beautiful white dress the night before, and Keith said seeing his young daughter dressed so beautifully had made it "well worth the trip."

They got the engine off the truck, and it was now 3 p.m. Keith suggested they call it a day and go cook up a big meal down at the cabins. It had been a long day for the men, and they eagerly climbed onto the A-frame truck. In their haste, they neglected to drag a log behind the vehicle, a common practice which served not only to bring one more log down the mountain, but also helped in the braking.

Another man took the wheel, and Keith hopped into the passenger's seat. The truck didn't have doors—just a windshield and a rollover bar. The driver took a short but steep road back to the cabins. As they started down the hill, the truck's drive line broke loose again.

The truck sideswiped a tree, and the driver steered toward a small hill to stop the truck. As the truck left the road, Keith was thrown to the ground. The truck's back right tire rolled over him, crushing his chest.

His fellow workers made their best efforts to revive him and get him breathing, but to no avail. Keith was taken from this earth and returned to his heavenly home.

His death at age 32 stunned the family and community. After proper care at Berg Mortuary, Keith's body was taken to his home and placed in the living room, where family and friends could pay their respects and offer sympathy. As was the tradition, a light was left on near the casket throughout the night.

On the morning of August 13, Keith's funeral was held at their church. The chapel was filled to capacity, and dozens of additional mourners filled the basement, where they could hear the service. Following the funeral, the procession traveled south about a mile to the Springville Evergreen Cemetery, where Keith's body was laid to rest with full military honors on a sloping hillside with a beautiful view of the valley.

On December 16, 1952, Rosalie and the children traveled to the Salt Lake Temple, where Rosalie and Keith (through proxy) received their endowments and were sealed for eternity. Then the children were sealed to their parents, preparing for that day when the family would once again be reunited.

CHAPTER THREE

❧

Son of a Steelworker

During the commotion surrounding Keith's death and funeral, little three-year-old Jack was feeling very confused. The night before, his father had lain in the front room without moving, and Jack had begged, "Daddy, wake up!"

Life suddenly became very challenging for Rosalie and her children. They didn't have life insurance, and although her parents helped out as much as they could, Rosalie saved every penny to make ends meet.

So although my dad Jack had a rambunctious childhood filled with pranks and troublemaking, he made it through okay. Rosalie eventually married a fine man named Glen Kirkwood who worked for the Provo School District, and money wasn't so tight anymore.

Dad's recreational outlet in life was his love for hunting and fishing. He also met a lovely young woman a year younger than him named Sheila Chesnut. They dated steadily throughout high school and even after Dad attended BYU. He was planning on serving a mission, but the events of the late 1960s sent my parents' lives in a different direction.

The United States government held a draft lottery, in which the draft order for American young men would be determined

My parents Jack Daybell and Sheila Chesnut during their high school days. What a good-looking couple!

randomly based on their birthdays. Dad's birthday was one of the first ones selected, meaning it was certain he would be drafted and be assigned to ground warfare in Vietnam.

A mission was no longer an option. The government was only allowing two missionaries per LDS ward to serve each year, and there were already several young men ahead of Dad on the list.

After his World War II experiences, Keith had told Rosalie that if their sons ever had to fight in a war, that they should try to get in the Navy or the Air Force where they would at least have a bed to sleep in at night. When Rosalie reminded Dad of that counsel, he decided to join the Naval Reserve.

Dad learned he would be stationed in San Diego, California, for at least two years. Mom's father Guy had served in the Navy in World War II and knew what Navy life could be like for a single sailor. He suggested they get married before Dad left for California.

My parents followed his advice. Rather than be separated,

they were married in the Logan Temple the summer after Mom graduated from high school. Then they headed to a new adventure in San Diego.

I Make My Earthly Debut

I was born a year later in Provo, Utah during Dad's two-week shore leave. My parents scheduled the shore leave to coincide with my due date and traveled to Utah so I could be born among family members. But my due date passed, and then another week slipped by. I still wasn't budging, though, and Dad needed to return to California in a few days.

Dad finally asked Mom to go for a bumpy ride with him up in the mountains to see if it would jolt me into action. It was a little risky, but it worked! I was born the next day. I'm just glad my birthplace wasn't Hobble Creek Canyon!

I was given my baby blessing at Grandma Rosalie's home, and then we headed back to California. We lived in a small

My dad and I spending some quality time together in 1969 while he was home on shore leave from his service in the U.S. Navy.

apartment in National City. Dad was gone to sea for long stretches of time, so Mom and I would drive around southern California in our little Volkswagen Bug and see the sights.

A Return to Utah

When Dad's service in the Navy ended, we moved back to Springville. Dad was offered a job at Geneva Steel in the Coke Plant, where they turned coal into pure carbon called "coke" that was used in the steelmaking process. It was a tough, dirty job, but my brother Paul had joined the family, so Dad did what he needed to do to support us.

Dad was soon selected by Geneva to complete an electrician apprenticeship through Utah Technical College, so during the mid-1970s he worked full-time, went to school all day Saturday, and squeezed in time for homework. He often had to work graveyard shifts, so he put a small cot in our cold concrete cellar and would sleep there during the day because we were so noisy.

As a young child I didn't understand how brutal his schedule was, but he graduated with straight A's and was promoted to a much-better job as an electrician.

As part of his work duties, Dad would go out at 2 a.m. and check various pieces of electrical equipment. His usual route included walking down a set of railroad tracks that went through a tunnel. This tunnel went under a building where coke was loaded into railroad cars.

One night, Dad walked about 30 feet into the tunnel when he heard a voice say, "Don't go through there."

He stopped for a second, thinking he was just being spooked. After all, it was an eerie place to walk around alone in the middle of the night. He laughed at himself, but only walked a few feet farther when a louder voice repeated, "Don't go through there."

He stopped again, but told himself to not be so nervous.

Then a loud voice said, "Jack, don't go through there!"

This third warning scared him enough that he retraced his steps out of the tunnel entrance and instead used the asphalt road that paralleled the tunnel.

He reached the other end of the tunnel and walked back onto the railroad rails. Just then there was a tremendous crash right behind him. A thick cloud of coke dust hit him and he couldn't see anything.

It took a minute for the dust to clear, then he saw a 40-foot-long conveyor belt system—with all of the structural steel supporting it—had fallen from 20 feet above the ground. It landed on the tracks where he would have been walking if he hadn't followed that prompting.

Company investigators discovered that a large cable that had been supporting the equipment for 30 years failed at that moment. Dad felt his father Keith was watching over him to save his life.

Over the years Dad continued to work his way up through the ranks at Geneva Steel, eventually becoming the General Manager of the Coke Plant. It wasn't a fun place to work, and the co-workers could often be tough to work with, but throughout the years I've met many men who worked with my dad, and they universally praise him for being such a good boss.

Changing Priorities

Dad was active in the Church as a teenager, and as I mentioned earlier, he had planned on serving a mission. However, as he juggled his many responsibilities at this time in his life, he didn't make it to Church very often. Sunday was Dad's only free day all week, and he sometimes relaxed by going hunting or fishing while Mom took us to church.

Apparently I had noticed, because when I was five years old

I asked Mom, "Why doesn't Daddy come to church?"

Mom shared my question with Dad, and he realized it was time for him to fully commit to Church activity. He began reading the Book of Mormon and had a very sacred experience that he holds close to his heart. He made the commitment to attend church each week.

That was a turning point in my life as well. It meant a lot to me to have Dad sitting in Sacrament Meeting with us. He was soon called to serve as the Teachers Quorum Advisor, and he had an immediate positive influence in the lives of several young men. They are still his close friends 40 years later.

My kindergarten photo in 1973, taken at Springville's Grant Elementary School .

CHAPTER FOUR

✦

Early Experiences

My first encounter with death came in third grade when my classmate Randy Perkins was helping his brother dig a cave in the foothills above town. The cave collapsed on him, and he suffocated before his brother could get him out. It was quite a shock to me and our entire school. They said Randy was now in heaven, but I didn't really understand what that meant. Death became a scary topic to me.

Sports became my main focus. Our neighborhood was filled with good athletes, and when we weren't playing in organized city leagues, we were playing pick-up games.

It really was a small-town, simplistic upbringing, and thankfully it kept us out of any real trouble. I was a year or two younger than most of the neighbor boys, so I had to continually improve my game to keep up with them.

I played Tee-Ball as an eight-year-old, and Dad was the coach. I played first base and we won every game.

My first year in Mustang League came to a screeching halt for me early in the season. I tried to score from third on a wild pitch. The catcher grabbed the ball and rushed back to tag me, so I slid awkwardly and banged my knee hard against the corner of home plate.

My knee was tingling, so I pulled up my pant leg and nearly fainted at the sight. I had cut my knee to the kneecap. Then I bent my knee in fright, splitting the skin to the back of my knee, exposing the muscles and tendons as well. It was quite gory, but it wasn't bleeding.

Dad had been coaching third base, and he hurried over to me. He took one look at it, scooped me up, and carried me to our truck before speeding to Utah Valley Hospital in Provo. It took 80 stitches to close the wound (40 deep inside the knee, and another 40 outside). The doctors gave me a leg brace and wrapped it up tightly. They told me to stay off of it and to not even bump it for at least a month.

Well, a week later at my grandparents' home we had a Fourth of July party and my cousins were playing kickball. I couldn't resist playing, and I fell directly on my injured knee. The impact with the ground tore out all of those stitches.

I rolled over and watched the gauze around my knee instantly turn bright red. My cousins all freaked out, and then it was essentially a repeat of the first time, with Dad rushing me to the car and hurrying me to the emergency room again.

Mom sat with me this time in the back seat, applying cloths to my knee, but it just kept bleeding. I lost a lot of blood and the skin was badly damaged from the stitches ripping out. I was now under strict orders to stay on the couch for the rest of the summer.

This was in early June, and I dreaded the long summer ahead of me. Thankfully my aunt Sue Creer bought me a couple of *Hardy Boys* books. I read those two books and got hooked on the series. Over the next year, I read every *Hardy Boys* book in print, and I also read the entire *Alfred Hitchcock and the Three Investigators* series.

The knee injury was horrible, but it allowed me to develop a love of reading, which I might not have happened if I'd been playing sports all summer. Once I healed up, I began making regular visits to the Springville Library, and over the years I've read hundreds of novels.

All of this reading sparked a desire within me to give writing a try. In fourth grade I handwrote a short novel entitled *The Murder of Dr. Jay and His Assistant*. My teacher Mr. Bushman really liked it, and he had a school employee type it up. It was a fun story—despite the gruesome title—and they put it in the school library so my friends could check it out to read. I even received a commendation letter from the Nebo School District Superintendent. I suppose it was a foreshadowing of my future career.

Babe Ruth Jr.

By the next summer my knee was fully recovered, although I had a nasty scar that I still carry.

I had a bit of a chip on my shoulder about the way the previous season had ended. Plus, I had grown a lot and was one of the biggest kids in the league. I was used to playing with the older neighbor boys, so this season almost seemed too easy.

To top it off, Mom offered me a silver dollar for every home run I hit. I didn't need the extra motivation, but I wasn't going to turn her down, either.

It admittedly got a little ridiculous. The baseball fields we played on didn't have outfield fences, so all I had to do was hit a long line drive between the outfielders and I would circle the bases before they even grabbed the ball. Some coaches tried to pitch around me, but I'd sometimes chase a bad pitch and still crush it.

I ended up with 38 silver dollars in 10 games, and I definitely needed some humbling. Don't worry, the Lord had a plan in mind.

My first and still most-imposing book cover. The teacher's aide who put it together really created a classic. And no, the bird isn't the killer.

Over the next three years I noticed how other kids were really sprouting up. At first I didn't think much about it, but then it dawned on me I had hardly grown since that memorable baseball season. I'd been just over 5 feet tall that year, and now entering seventh grade I was the same height!

My grandma Rosalie was only 4'11", and my dad is 5'9" on a good day, so I realized my fate as a short person might be sealed.

I continued to play sports, but I certainly wasn't the head of the class anymore. Little did I know that my grade contained the greatest collection of athletes Springville has ever seen.

Our middle school coach told us we would be lucky if one player from our grade played college football, but from that group of about 150 boys we had 14 college athletes and one NFL quarterback, who I will discuss later.

Matt Nearly Gets Shot

Dad would often take me hunting with him. During the pheasant hunt of 1980, I was the only child old enough to actually shoot a gun, but my younger brothers Paul and Matt had begged to come, too. We loaded the hunting dogs in the truck, then my brothers and I piled into the cab. However, Dad was still at the doorway.

"Boys, aren't we forgetting something? Come back in and let's have a family prayer," he said.

We all knelt around the couch and listened as Dad prayed that we would be protected that day during our hunt.

Following the prayer, we drove to an area west of Genola, Utah, and began walking slowly through a field, waiting for the dogs to scare up some pheasants.

I loaded in a shell and excitedly waited for a pheasant to fly up. Paul and Matt trailed behind Dad and me. We came to a ditch, and Matt ran ahead and jumped across first. He landed on the other side and scared up a rooster pheasant in the process.

I quickly put the gun to my shoulder and got the pheasant aligned in my gun sight just as Matt stood up on the other side of the ditch. His head was only a few feet from the end of my barrel. In my excitement, I hadn't noticed him. All I heard was my Dad and Paul shouting, "No, Matt, no!"

It was too late—I had pulled the trigger. We all heard the gun click, but the shot was not fired. Dad dropped to his knees in shock while we stood in silence.

Finally Dad stood and took my gun. He popped the shell out of the chamber and examined it. The shell's primer, which is hit by a hammer to spark the gunpowder, was deeply indented. The gun should have fired and Matt should have been killed instantly.

We prayed again in that field, thanking the Lord for preserving Matt's life, and for fulfilling Dad's humble prayer earlier that morning.

Eighth Grade Troubles

If Matt had died, it would have really sent me into a tailspin, because by the time I started eighth grade at the junior high I was basically mad at the world. The friends I had previously walked to middle school with now took a different route to the junior high, and it felt like I didn't have any friends.

In my woodshop class, I became the target of a bully. He sat right next to me, and whenever the teacher left the room, this kid would just pound his fists into my shoulder and back. I finally told the teacher what was happening, and he moved the kid away from me, but my self-esteem was pretty low.

One day that spring I was slowly walking home across Memorial Park after school, and I saw a honeybee pollinating a dandelion. I peered at it for a moment, then smashed it with my shoe. I spotted another one, then another one. I got a strange satisfaction from it. I kept count, and after about a half hour I had killed 120 bees. Then as I was about to step on another bee, a masculine voice shouted in my ear, "Hey! Stop it! Leave them alone!"

I jumped back and looked around, but there wasn't anyone in sight. I was really shook up, because the man had sounded really angry. I walked in a circle for a minute, trying to make sense of it. Finally I realized that maybe an angel was fed up with me killing God's innocent creatures.

That incident helped me realize how pathetic I had become, and I decided to start making some better choices.

I love the comparison of these two photos. In the top one I'm No. 14, and this is the season when I smacked 38 home runs. In the bottom photo I'm No. 40, which was taken nearly three years later. I'm the same height in both photos! I'm actually taller now than those long-haired giants behind me.

CHAPTER FIVE

Finding My Religion

I had been ordained a deacon the previous year, but I really didn't study the gospel. I had received some handheld electronic sports games for Christmas, and that's how I spent most of my time after school.

Then came the "bee" chastisement. I'd never been yelled at by an unseen voice before, and I didn't want it to occur again. I started setting some goals. One goal was to read the Book of Mormon. My Deacons quorum advisor had encouraged me to read it, so I finally opened up the book and slowly made my way through it. The Isaiah chapters in Second Nephi really baffled me, but I pushed forward. Once I reached the book of Alma I was really enjoying the story.

Interestingly, I had started reading non-LDS religious books from the library at the same time. I was still learning about the doctrines of the gospel, and I wasn't sure how everything fit together.

I checked out a book from the library that talked about reincarnation and past lives, and I can remember the dark feelings the book generated in me. I knew the Spirit was telling me, "This is false."

I returned the book and focused solely on finishing the Book of Mormon. I knew we would be studying it in ninth-grade Seminary, so I figured I would at least be ahead of the class.

When I finished reading the Book of Mormon, I wanted the spiritual confirmation that the prophet Moroni talked about at the end of the book. I knew Joseph Smith had prayed in a grove of trees, so I went into a field behind our house with tall grass and prayed for a while, but all I got was a bunch of ant bites on my legs.

I reasoned that maybe it needed to be more challenging, so during a rainstorm I kneeled in the mud in the backyard and prayed for 20 minutes, but all I received was a good drenching.

Deep down I knew the book was true and felt good when I read it, but I suppose I expected something along the lines of a heavenly messenger appearing to me.

Finally one day when I was praying in my bedroom, I got the impression to write in my journal. As I started to do so, the Spirit rushed into the room. My chest was burning with a confirmation about the truthfulness of the Book of Mormon, and I was able to write my feelings down as this occurred.

The Spirit was so powerful that I started crying. As I described the experience, I wrote, "Thank you, Heavenly Father! I know without a doubt that the Book of Mormon is true!"

Attending General Conference

That answered prayer was the beginning of my personal spiritual awakening. Later that year one of my Aaronic Priesthood leaders asked our quorum members if we would like to attend General Conference. He told us he knew how to get front-row seats in the Salt Lake Tabernacle for the Priesthood Session, and that we'd get to shake hands with the General Authorities. He said it would require the sacrifice of standing in line for several hours, but he promised it would be worth it.

On the first Saturday in April, we arrived at Temple Square at 9:30 a.m. and stood next to a certain tree near the northeast corner of the Tabernacle. Once the doors closed for the 10 a.m. session, our leader walked over and spoke to an usher at one of the side doors, who nodded and waved to us. That was it. We were the first ones in line for the Priesthood Session.

We were able to take a few breaks and stretch our legs, as long as most of our group stayed in line. We listened to the two Saturday sessions, and then at 5 p.m. the usher allowed us into the Tabernacle. We were front and center, sitting only a few feet away from where the General Authorities would be seated facing us.

At about 5:15, several of the General Authorities came back into the Tabernacle. Rather than taking their seats on the stand, they came down into the congregation to greet us. It was wonderful to shake their hands and spend a few seconds conversing with each one of them.

The conversation that has stuck with me the most was with Elder Bruce R. McConkie. I had only seen him give stern, loud talks that seemingly rattled the pulpit. So I was a little intimidated, but when I told him where I was from, he gave me the biggest smile and said he loved visiting Springville.

Once the apostles took their seats, the Seventies did as well, and sitting directly across from me was Elder Angel Abrea from Argentina, who had just been sustained as a General Authority earlier that day. He motioned me toward him, so I stood up and shook his hand. He asked, "Is this your first time at Conference?"

I nodded, and he said, "I'm glad you're here. This is where the Lord wants you to be."

Our Aaronic Priesthood group made it a tradition to get the front row for the next few conferences, and each time Elder Abrea would motion for me to come forward and chat. It was like having a General Authority penpal that I would catch up with every six months. It was an exciting surprise to open the November 1981 Ensign magazine and see a photo of my friend Rob Barrus and I talking to Elder Abrea.

A Change in Perspective

A key turning point in my life came in 1982 I received my Patriarchal Blessing from Ray Cope, our stake patriarch. At that time, most teenagers were waiting until they were at least 16 before receiving their blessings, but I had a strong feeling that I should get mine at 14.

Admittedly, the song "Only the Good Die Young" by Billy Joel had strangely affected me, and I started wondering if I was going to die young, because I was doing my best to live the gospel.

Thankfully the blessing made it clear I had a long, wonderful life ahead of me, and it was very comforting. It spoke about serving a mission, going to college, marrying a wonderful woman and raising a strong family. It also mentioned spiritual gifts that would be made known to me later in life that I would cultivate to bless the lives of others.

It really gave me hope and opened my mind to life's possibilities, because prior to that time I fully expected to graduate from high school and then work at Geneva Steel until retirement. After all, Dad was following that route, and a lot of my relatives had as well.

I had just assumed that I would be expected to become an electrician like my father. Around that time I had asked him, "Dad, what if I don't want to become an electrician?"

He chuckled a little and said, "I don't expect you to become one. Get good grades, go to college, and become whatever you want to be."

His comment really surprised me. I'm definitely not

mechanically minded, so I was greatly relieved.

Dad was called to serve in our ward's High Priest Group leadership at around this time, and our family gathered at the Springville Stake offices for him to be ordained. Grandma Rosalie joined us, and I sat next to her a couple of rows back. On the other side of her was a vacant chair against the wall.

As we waited for the stake president to arrive, I noticed Grandma kind of jump in her chair. She smiled slightly and looked toward the vacant chair.

I turned and gave her a curious look, and she looked around a moment to see if anyone else was listening. Then she whispered in my ear, "Your Grandpa Keith is sitting next to me."

I looked over and didn't see anything, of course, but a week or so later I rode my bike over to Grandma's house and asked her about it. She told me that she felt his presence often, and that he attended a lot of family events. She wasn't surprised that Grandpa Keith had been in attendance at Dad's ordination.

At this time, Dad was trying to sort out in his mind how Keith had been killed. Dad had grown up thinking that the accident happened several miles away, above the town of Kamas. The members of the logging crew had told that story to Rosalie so she wouldn't have bad thoughts about the sawmill site in Soapstone Basin in the Uinta Mountains.

She in turn, told the same story to Dad about Keith dying near Kamas. Since Grandma didn't know the real location, it allowed the family to still have picnics and reunions at the logging site without negative feelings.

One summer, Dad took our family camping to the sawmill site. There was still a large sawdust pile there from the days of the logging camp, and while we played there, Dad took a short hike alone. He walked up the dirt road to the slope above the sawdust pile and looked at a place where they had loaded logs onto trailers. As he started walking back down the road to rejoin us, he started getting a strange feeling that this road was where Keith had died. He was very confused, because it didn't match the story he had always been told.

The thought "my father died here" came stronger into his mind. As he walked down the hill to the spot where Keith had been run over, Dad was overcome with emotion. He felt so weak that he dropped to his knees. He knew this was the exact place his father had died. He knelt there crying for some time before finally gathering enough strength to walk back to our camp and tell us about his experience.

Dad later asked his older brother Ray what he knew about the accident, and Ray confirmed it had happened at that spot. Another man who had been injured in the accident was still alive, and he also told Dad that it had occurred there, along with other important details.

Dad feels that Keith was there that day to help him better understand what actually happened, for whatever reason, even if it was just to let him know he is there helping when he can.

Helping Milt Harrison

Two people I got to know quite well growing up were Milt and Leah Harrison, who lived around the corner from us. They had allowed us to play football and baseball in their big backyard over the years.

Milt was confined to a wheelchair. He had developed polio as a young man, and now in his 80s his legs had completely stopped working.

One day Leah called our home and asked if my parents and I could visit them. When we arrived, Leah broke into tears. She said Milt's strength was ebbing away, and she wasn't strong enough to lift him in and out of bed by herself.

"Would it be possible for Chad to come help Milt each

morning and night?" Leah asked. "It will only take a few minutes, and I can pay you a dollar a day."

My parents felt good about it, but they left the decision up to me. I looked into Milt and Leah's eyes, and it was like seeing old friends. I nodded, and Leah clapped her hands.

"Thank you," she said. "This will be such a blessing to us."

That began a daily odyssey for me from age 14 until Milt's death when I was 17. I went each day before school to help him get dressed and into his wheelchair. Then we'd reverse the process each night. It would take about 10 minutes each visit.

When I started helping Milt, he didn't warm up to me very quickly. I think it had more to do with letting someone take care of him, rather than anything to do with me. I forever cracked his cold scowl, though, when I asked, "What was it like around here when you were a boy?"

Over the next few years I probably heard 1,000 different stories, because Milt rarely repeated himself and would remember where he left off the day before. It was like stepping back into Springville's history. Milt was born in 1900, and his grandfather owned the Harrison Hotel on Springville's Main Street. This was long before the freeway system, so travelers would pass through each town along the Wasatch Front.

The Harrison Hotel was considered a high-class institution, and many prominent people stayed there and ate in the hotel's dining room, whether they traveled by train or by wagon.

As a young teenager, Milt would help out with the hotel chores, but his grandpa would make a point to introduce him to the famous visitors who would stop there. Milt felt honored to haul the luggage of prophets and apostles to their rooms.

Milt told me he felt a special connection to Joseph F. Smith, who was the prophet at the time. Whenever the prophet spoke in Springville, Milt did his best to be on the chapel's front row, and the prophet would make a point to shake Milt's hand.

By this time I had heard the story of Finity Daybell defending Joseph F. Smith in England, and it kind of blew my mind that both Finity and Milt had met President Smith. I realize now how fortunate I was to become friends with Milt. He provided me a link to the early days of the Church that the rising generation doesn't have.

Milt gave me a lot of advice about life. Some of it I heeded, while other times I just smiled to myself. For example, he and Leah hadn't gotten married until their late 30s, so he was pretty adamant that I didn't need to go on any dates until after my mission.

Since I had to help Milt each night at 9 p.m., he did actually curtail my social life, but it was a blessing in disguise that helped keep me out of trouble. My friends were quite understanding, and they all got to know Milt and Leah and would substitute for me if our family went on vacation. It was an invaluable experience for me.

A Curious Visitor in the Manti Temple

My mother's side of the family is also filled with humble Church members who paved the way for me.

At around the time I started helping Milt, my Grandpa Guy Chesnut sat me down and told me an amazing story of what happened to him in the Manti Temple. It opened my mind to how our ancestors in the Spirit World are very aware of what we are doing on earth.

Life didn't start out easily for Grandpa. He was born in 1923 to Alma and Almira Chesnut in the tiny town of Teasdale in southern Utah. He weighed 13.5 pounds at birth. Three weeks later Almira passed away, and suddenly Alma was a single father with six children.

The Oyler family heard about Alma's predicament, and asked

if they could take in the motherless newborn. The Oylers were converts to the LDS Church and lived in Fruita, which is now inside Capitol Reef National Park.

Their homestead is now gone, but it was at the base of a stone cliff that contains Native American petroglyphs and is a popular tourist spot. There's a sign that reads "Tyne Oyler Place" at that location.

Guy attended the small one-room schoolhouse that is along Highway 24. There's a recorded message from a former schoolteacher who mentions a student putting a snake in her desk drawer, giving her a good scare. That was him!

He worked hard on the Oyler farm and became a key part of their family. He even took their last name, and was known as Guy Oyler.

When he reached ninth grade he left the small school in Fruita and began attending school at Wayne High in Bicknell. One day the gym teacher brought in a man who had been a professional boxer to teach the boys to defend themselves. After demonstrating a few techniques, the boxer selected Guy to be his opponent. As they began circling each other, Guy faked with his left hand, then knocked the boxer to the ground with a solid right-hand punch to the face. That quickly ended the day's boxing demonstration.

Guy made the varsity basketball team his junior year, but as the team began its preseason schedule, Guy became very ill. He woke up one day to discover he was paralyzed from the waist down. The doctor diagnosed the illness as polio, and Guy was told he would never walk again. But through, faith, prayers, and determination, he was on his feet in three months. He was using crutches at first, but he soon discarded them.

During this time Guy became acquainted with a pretty, dark-haired girl named Flora Chappell. After a year of steady dating they were married in 1943. World War II was raging, and four days after their marriage Guy departed for eight weeks of Navy boot camp. This was followed by an assignment on the USS Pocomoke, where he served as a medical corpsman. His ship traveled throughout the South Pacific and participated in every major military campaign there.

He returned safely home and worked a variety of jobs. He owned his own long-haul truck, but eventually started painting houses to be at home. He developed his skills and became a leader in the industry, where he was known for his honesty and hard work. He later expanded his operation and began building homes.

An important moment in my grandparents' lives came during a visit to the Manti Temple in the late 1940s.

As Guy and Flora were walking in the main hallway of the temple, a man approached who they had never met. The man stepped in front of Guy and asked, "Who's your father?"

"Al Chesnut," Guy replied.

"I've seen your father," the man said. "You look like him."

The man then smiled and asked, "Have you done your genealogy?"

"No, I've had a hard time tracing my father's line," Guy said.

The man nodded. "I know who can help you."

The stranger then named a man in Helper, Utah who would have the records they needed. Flora searched through her purse for something to write down the name on, and Guy turned to help her. When they turned back, the man was gone and the hallway was empty.

In the split second they had taken their eyes off the man, he had disappeared. Guy rushed to the nearest doorway, but the stranger wasn't there. They wanted to thank him, but he wasn't anywhere to be found. No one in the temple recalled seeing a man matching his description.

The man was dressed in a typical suit and didn't appear any

different than other men, but it seems a messenger from heaven had been sent to help Guy find his genealogy. This came as a surprise to Guy, because up to that point in his life he had come to think of himself as an "Oyler."

Guy contacted the man in Helper, and he found out a great deal of information on his ancestors. Guy and Flora were able to do the temple work for dozens of Guy's relatives, and to trace his line back to the royalty of England. Without the prompting from this messenger, Guy may have never completed the temple work for his Chesnut ancestors.

My grandparents had five daughters who all reached teenagehood in the 1960s. They endured it well, and that alone should assure them direct admission to the Celestial Kingdom. The daughters all got married within a few years of each other, and Grandpa became a second father to his five new sons-in-law. I know Grandpa's influence played a huge role in helping my parents establish a happy marriage. He was the patriarch to a rapidly growing group of grandchildren, and he made each of us feel special.

Both Grandpa and Grandma have passed away, but I know they are busy in the Spirit World. Interestingly, after their passing, my mom suddenly became very interested in her family line, and she has since done the temple work for thousands of ancestral cousins. She knows her parents are inspiring her to find these people.

The Chesnut family in the early 1970s. My grandma Flora and grandpa Guy are seated in front, and from the left are my aunts Sue Creer, Vicki Murray, Teresa Miller, Evelyn Jensen, and my mom Sheila Daybell. My aunts have always been so supportive of me!

CHAPTER SIX

✧

Gaining My Footing in Life

My life began to improve the summer after eighth grade, even though my best friend was an 83-year-old man. I started growing taller again after a two-year pause, although now I had a lot of catching up to do.

A crucial point in my life came on the first day of ninth grade. During P.E. class as we listened to the coach talk, I noticed a tall boy that I'd met briefly at a family reunion a couple of weeks earlier. All I knew was that his name was Les, he'd just moved to Springville from Texas, and he was my mom's cousin.

As the class ended, I saw him go out into the hallway and turn left. My next class was to the right, but I had a strong impulse to chase him down. He was walking pretty fast, but I caught up to him and tapped him on the back.

"Hey, how's it going?" I asked.

Les turned to look at me, and a wave of relief passed over his face. "Hey! You're Chad, right?"

"Yeah, we have P.E. together."

We agreed to go to my house to play basketball after school that day, and that began the most important friendship of my life. It turned out Les was very good at basketball, but even better, he was very spiritual. We had both been looking for a friend to help us maintain our standards, and the Lord brought us together.

Les had a nice Datsun 280Z that we would cruise around town in. People probably thought we were looking for girls, but in reality we were discussing the Plan of Salvation. We were basically gospel nerds, but it was great. We encouraged each other to read the Book of Mormon once a year until our missions, and we did.

Once basketball season started, Les became a bonafide superstar on the court. He started on Springville High's varsity team as a sophomore and was a key part of the team's run to the state championship game. His junior-year performance was even better, and by the time we were seniors he had been named to several All-State teams.

The great thing about Les is he's a better person than he is a basketball player. Our friendship had nothing to do with athletics, and I think hanging out with me helped him keep the basketball hoopla in perspective.

We were able to do a lot together after we returned from our missions, and even now we can get together and talk just like old times. Everyone deserves to have a best friend like Les Chappell, and fortunately I do.

An End to My Sports Career

As I mentioned earlier, our class of 1986 was loaded with athletes. Scott Mitchell would lead us to Springville's only undefeated football season. He would go on to have great success as a quarterback in college and the pros.

Les and Scott were legitimately famous in our sports-crazy small town, but they always kept their heads on straight. It was an honor to grow up with both of them.

As for my own sports career, I had given up on football, and

I wasn't good enough to make the basketball team, but I had continued playing on the high school baseball teams.

During my junior year I was the JV starting centerfielder, and I started out hot, hitting .750 through the first few games. I eventually cooled off, but they moved me up to the varsity team for the state playoffs. We reached the championship game at the old Derks Field in Salt Lake, but our pitchers were worn out, and American Fork was hammering us.

The game was basically over, so our coach let me bat in the last inning. I got up with two outs and hit a hard one-hopper to their shortstop. He threw me out by a step at first base, and suddenly I was surrounded by the American Fork players as they celebrated their state championship. I fought my way through them and got ready for a sad bus ride home.

Springville would win the state title the next year, but I wasn't on the team. Why? Because I had jumped off a cliff at Flaming Gorge the summer before my senior year, and suddenly sports just didn't hold my interest anymore.

An Eventful Senior Year

One of the beneficial side effects of nearly dying at Flaming Gorge was I became more outgoing. I was appointed as the Student Council Treasurer, and it kept me so busy that I didn't focus much on my recent near-death experience.

We had a slightly crazy group on the Student Council, and we had one goal for our assemblies—keep the students entertained. Every assembly turned into a major production. My favorite skit was when I performed as a rock star and jumped off the stage into the crowd.

I played a major role in the Homecoming Assembly, since my dad had graduated exactly 20 years earlier. He and I did a skit where he acted like a senile old man, and I was supposed to slap him back to reality. We hadn't rehearsed the slap, but when I slapped him in the assembly, I caught him just right and it sounded really loud. I hadn't hurt him, but he played it up nicely and had the crowd wondering if he was going to punch me out.

School Success

My senior year we had to write a "technical writing" essay on how to perform a certain task. I wrote mine on helping Milt, with the catchy title of "How to Put an Old Man to Bed." I took third place in the state and got to attend a fancy banquet in Salt Lake to receive a certificate. Milt was as proud as anyone.

That essay was part of the reason I was named Springville High's Sterling Scholar in English, but I really didn't have the credentials to match the students from other schools.

I was eliminated in the first round. It didn't help that at the end of my less-than-impressive interview with the judges, they asked if I had anything else to add. I shrugged and said, "Nope, that's about it."

I graduated from Springville High School with high honors, and really just had a fun time that year. I was awarded a two-year full-tuition BYU Presidential scholarship, which was a great blessing.

Trouble with the Law

Like most teenagers, I still had a few episodes of stupidity. This one tops the list. One night three friends and I were driving around a neighborhood where a sophomore girl was having a birthday party.

One of the friends is now a prominent surgeon and wasn't really the instigator anyway, so I won't use his name. But the other two, Daren and Chris, still love to tell the story and deserve the blame anyway.

We began our adventure by throwing tomatoes and onions

at the girl's house from a nearby school field, but we didn't quite have the arm strength. We could see our projectiles were only hitting the front lawn. The girls had noticed what was happening, and they had come out to pick up the vegetables.

One of the girls figured out where we must be. She came over toward the fence and called out, "You better stop, or her mom is going to make you regret it!"

That was the wrong thing to say to Daren and Chris. Before I knew it, they had loaded the remaining tomatoes into Daren's Blazer, and we were driving slowly down that street. As we passed the house, Chris lobbed a big juicy tomato at the front window, and it splattered perfectly.

As we laughingly drove away, I figured we were done for the night, but Daren circled around and went past the house one more time. Suddenly a car's headlights popped on in the driveway, and I could see the girl's mom in the drivers seat. Daren floored it, but she was right on our tail.

For the next fifteen minutes she chased us all over southern Springville. We reached speeds of at least 70 miles per hour down residential streets, and there was more than one time we were on two wheels going around corners.

I was in the back seat holding on for dear life while keeping an eye on the mom. She nearly wrecked three times trying to keep up before she finally backed off and disappeared. We couldn't believe we escaped.

We were now within a couple of blocks of Daren's house. I thought I spotted a police car behind us, so Daren turned off his headlights and pulled into a vacant field. Our hearts dropped as the policeman pulled into the field and turned on his flashing lights. He just sat in his car, and we stayed put too.

Then we heard sirens coming from all over town. Within two minutes there were not one, not two, but six police cars surrounding us. Until then I didn't even know Springville had that many police cars. Each officer exited his car with his gun drawn and pointed at us.

As they approached, one of the officers yelled, "Put your hands up where we can see them!"

We recognized the voice. It was one of our seminary teachers who worked nights as a police officer. We were doomed.

He shined a powerful flashlight on each of our faces then gave an irritated shout to his fellow officers. "Congratulations, guys! We've just captured the freaking Springville High Seminary Council!"

The next half-hour didn't go too favorably for us. The officers lashed into us pretty good. We avoided actual arrest, but it would have been preferable to what came next.

With a police car in front and behind us, we returned to the girl's house in Daren's vehicle. Her parents and the girls were waiting on the front lawn, and there wasn't a smile to be seen. The policemen motioned for us to get out, and then they led us to stand in front of the girl's parents.

We each mumbled our apologies and kept our heads low, but her dad recognized me. He growled, "Daybell! What in the world were you thinking?!?"

I didn't have an answer. Then he said, "Well, the girls cleaned up your mess. You better thank them."

So we had to move down the line and apologize to the girls too. Finally they let us slink away.

The hardest part was still to come. It was now after midnight, and my parents were asleep. I woke them up, though, and said, "Um, you might hear something about me around town tomorrow . . ."

Above: The Daybell family in 1986. My parents in the back with my brother Matt, and then along the front is Brad, me, Paul and Becky.

Right: My senior class photo, taken in 1986.

age 17

Born 1969
age 48 2017
I'm 16 1953
older
Have 6 1980
age Boy
Boy 4 1984

2018
1969
48

age 17 – 1986
48 – 2017
49 – 2018

CHAPTER SEVEN

Freshman Frustration at BYU

Milt passed away the summer after I graduated, and it left a fairly big void in my life. I was still only 17, so I worked for the Springville City Parks Department that summer then arranged to attend BYU for a full year before serving my mission.

When I started college at BYU that fall, I continued to live at home, but it was admittedly a lonely time. My friend Les Chappell had gone to Utah Valley State College on a basketball scholarship, so we really didn't cross paths too often anymore.

I had other friends who were at BYU, but they were also very busy, and many of them left on their missions after the fall semester.

I vividly remember walking slowly across the BYU campus during a January snowstorm and thinking, "There isn't a soul on earth who cares what I'm doing right now."

I knew that statement wasn't completely true, but at home it seemed life revolved around my other siblings' activities, and at BYU I had taken General Education classes, meaning I was seated with hundreds of students in large auditoriums where I rarely sat by the same person twice.

My afternoons were usually spent studying so I could keep my scholarship. There were some cubicles tucked away on the fourth floor of the Harold B. Lee Library, and that's where I spent a lot of time when I wasn't in class. I actually preferred being on campus or at home, because that's where I felt the safest. During the hectic pace of my senior year, the issue of my newly torn veil didn't bother me too much. But once my life slowed down the following summer, I realized there were people in another realm who were very aware of me.

Some of them were friendly spirits, while others were definitely dark souls. They never approached me, but I was able to discern they were people who had lived in the area many years earlier. For some reason when they had died, they didn't go to the light. They had stayed behind on earth and now were stuck in limbo.

If they got too close to me, the hair on my head would stand on end. I tried to ignore them, because if I acknowledged them they seemed to hang around me a lot longer.

I found it interesting that these spirits weren't congregated in cemeteries, abandoned buildings, or quiet areas. Most of the time they were wherever there was a lot of human energy they could feed off. I went to a high school basketball game that winter, and there were dozens of them in attendance!

As I mentioned, I felt safe on the BYU campus, particularly in the old Joseph Smith Building. It was hallowed ground that had a protective spiritual barrier against wandering spirits.

Class Opposites

My favorite class during that year was an advanced religion course on the Pearl of Great Price. I had read a fascinating book about the earth written by BYU professor Rodney Turner, and I jumped at the chance to take a course from him.

The class consisted of 20 students, and most of them were married with two or three kids. I later realized the class was probably required for a major such as Old Testament Studies, but I thrived in it. Brother Turner could see I was soaking up this knowledge, and he would kindly spend a few minutes after each class answering my questions. His explanations helped me fit together God's eternal plan.

I regret not telling him about my cliff-jumping experience, because I think he would have appreciated it. I saw his obituary in the newspaper in 2014, and I'm sure he's loving life in the Spirit World.

On the opposite end of the spectrum was my freshman math class. Somehow my accident had made me even dumber when it came to math. It was as if any knowledge I had beyond basic multiplication had been erased.

Early in the semester we had an in-class test where you had to show your work. I had studied hard, but after twenty minutes I hadn't solved a single problem. I could envision my scholarship being ripped away because of failing that class.

As the minutes ticked away, I was on the verge of a panic attack. I finally walked up to the professor and asked him to come out into the hall with me. Once we were alone, I started crying. "I don't know what's wrong with me," I said. "I can't even do one problem right."

He was a gruff, older gentleman, and he could have easily said, "Tough luck, kid."

Instead, he put his hand on my shoulder and said, "It will be okay. Go ahead and take it home tonight and work on it. Use your book if you have to. Then bring it to me in the morning."

I was stunned. I hadn't expected that kind of compassion from him. I thanked him profusely, hurried back into the classroom to grab my backpack, then headed home.

Even with help from the book I only got an 88, but it sure beat getting a zero. That experience has come to my mind many times in recent years when it's been my turn to give someone a break.

"There's More to Life Than Utah Valley"

I dated a nice girl a few times that I'd met in my Communications 101 class, but we didn't really click. She was from Florida, and on our final date she said, "Sorry, but you need to get out and see the world. There's more to life than Utah Valley."

I was slightly offended. I mean, I'd been to Disneyland three times with my family, and one time I'd walked about a mile into Tijuana, Mexico. Then there was the trip to the Four Corners Monument where I'd stood in four different states at the same time! What did she mean I hadn't seen the world?

I was about to find out.

Submitting My Mission Papers Early

I was receiving strong promptings that February to submit my mission papers early. The standard practice at the time was to wait until three months before your 19th birthday to start working on them, which would have been in mid-May for me.

That felt way too late, so Dad and I talked to our bishop about it. The bishop was very reluctant to even consider it, saying he'd never seen anyone leave early, but he agreed to give it a try.

We took care of all the interviews and medical requirements, including removing four of my wisdom teeth, and we sent the papers to Church headquarters in March.

The bishop was pretty blunt with me that he felt this had been an unnecessary rush. He expected my papers to be returned and that he'd have to resend them at a later time. I just kept quiet, because I knew it had been the right thing to do.

BYU's semester ended, and I started working for the Parks Department again while I waited for my mission call. I came home for lunch one day in early May, and Mom met me at the door. She was acting frantic.

"What's going on?" I asked.

She shoved a big white envelope into my hand. "It's your mission call! Call your dad at work. Do you know how hard it has been for me to wait?"

Mom was doing a nervous little dance around the kitchen as I got Dad on the phone. Then I tore open the envelope and read, "You are assigned to labor in the New Jersey Morristown Mission. You should report to the Missionary Training Center in Provo, Utah on Wednesday, July 15, 1987. You will learn the discussions in Spanish."

Mom let out a scream, and I couldn't quite believe it, because I hadn't ever thought of New Jersey as a possible destination. I knew it was one of the 13 original colonies, but that was it.

Then Mom looked at the reporting date again. "July 15th! That's only two months away! We need to get busy."

We called the bishop, and he was surprised I'd received my call so early, but he was very happy for me.

Only later did I realize the full significance of the promptings to send my papers in early. At the time of my call, my mission didn't even exist yet. It was officially formed on July 1, 1987 as a division from the New York New York Mission.

This put me among the first group of Spanish-speaking missionaries called to the mission. We were going to take the gospel into some rough urban areas where it had never been preached before. Excitement was just around the corner!

CHAPTER EIGHT

Life in the Garden State

I had the usual emotional farewell with my family at the Missionary Training Center. The only hitch was the volunteers thought baby-faced Dad was also a missionary and nearly didn't let him leave.

I was on a spiritual high in the MTC, similar to when the energy particles had bombarded me during my near-death experience. Spiritual light was continually being poured through my torn veil. MTC President George Durrant's powerful talks always filled me with great enthusiasm, and I felt closer to the Savior there than ever before.

One time during our classroom study, our teacher shared with us a poem about the Savior leaving his heavenly home to suffer the indignities of earth life to die for us. As the teacher read it, I could visualize the scenes of what was happening in the poem, and I started sobbing in gratitude. I couldn't stop.

The teacher just stared at me as if to say, "Get a grip, man. It's just a poem."

Finally the teacher told the rest of my district to take a break, and he left me alone in the room as I got my emotions under control. I was embarrassed, but I was also exuberant. The Spirit had testified so strongly to me of the reality of Jesus Christ and that I had been called to spread the gospel. It was a fortifying moment that I would soon rely on.

"Don't Start Having Doubts"

After nine weeks of learning Spanish in the MTC, our group of six missionaries departed for New Jersey in mid-September. After a layover in Chicago, we arrived at Newark International Airport. The Assistants to the President picked us up, and started praising how beautiful the state was.

Then the driver took a wrong turn and we found ourselves driving through the outskirts of Newark and Jersey City before he got on the right freeway. We all looked at each other as if to say, "This place doesn't look too beautiful to me."

We finally arrived at the mission home in Morristown, and they had prepared a nice meal for us on the back patio, but I was sweating to death. I'd been warned about the humidity, but on this day it was almost unbearable.

Our mission president arrived that evening, and I finally started feeling comfortable. President Dan J. Workman and his wife Barbara are among the greatest people I have ever known. They showed genuine love and concern for me during my entire mission.

The next morning I met my companion, Elder Hansen. He was a confident Californian who spoke fluent Spanish. He was the right companion for me to cope with the culture shock. Our proselytizing area was the city of Paterson, but with only six Spanish-speaking companionships to begin with in the entire state, our area was actually northcentral New Jersey. At least we had a car!

As we got to Paterson, Elder Hansen said we had a teaching appointment to do even before we went to our apartment. He pulled off the freeway to a rundown four-plex with no grass.

The family didn't have air-conditioning, and the heat was claustrophobic in their apartment. We taught them the fourth discussion and read parts of the illustrated Book of Mormon reader with the two children, and then they served us orange juice and cookies. I guess it was a typical visit, but it quickly threw me right into the real world. My heart was heavy, and I was exhausted.

I quickly learned that average citizens there weren't as pleasant as they could be. While walking around Paterson the next day, I waved to a man sitting on a porch step, and 15 seconds later a couple of apples came whizzing past our heads. Friendly guy! Then I waved to a couple of young kids, and they each threw a bottle at us. That tells you how filthy the streets were if they could so easily locate a couple of bottles so quickly. I decided that waving to people might not be the best thing to do.

Then we walked to Branch President Salcedo's house. The only way to get there was along River Street, probably the worst street in town. Ahead of us, a gang of teenagers were goofing around, taking up the whole sidewalk, as if it was their territory. I was praying hard for protection, and somehow we made it around them with only a few snide comments.

When we got to the Salcedos' house, they weren't there, although we'd set up a visit with them the night before. When they didn't answer the door, I suddenly felt exasperated and overwhelmed, and it must have shown on my face. Elder Hansen stuck his index finger in my chest, pushed me against the wall and said, "Don't start having doubts, man. You know this is the true church, and that Joseph Smith was a prophet. Are you going to let a bunch of losers on the street corner change your mind? I thought you were bigger than that."

Then he started walking back to the street. I was humbled and humiliated, but I caught up with him. We didn't say a word to each other, but he had made a good point. An image of Peter denying Christ came into my head, and I suddenly felt very ashamed.

When we reached our apartment, I thanked Elder Hansen for what he'd said, but he just shrugged it off. But that night I went into the bathroom and prayed a fervent prayer to Heavenly Father, apologizing for my weaknesses. Then I gave thanks for the Prophet Joseph Smith, and suddenly my mind opened up, and I felt like I was actually witnessing the First Vision.

It wasn't portrayed as the paintings or movies depict it, but I knew this was how it really happened. I felt the Spirit burning within me, and I was grateful for such a witness. It was a day I'll always remember, because I experienced fear, exasperation, and even doubt, but then I received an outpouring of the Spirit.

An Unforgettable Little Boy

About a week later I did a missionary exchange in Newark with Elder Alvarado from Puerto Rico. We arrived at the missionaries' apartment, which was in the attic of a rundown house on one of the worst streets I've ever seen. It might have been nice in 1920, but now it was a trash heap. There was no grass in the parking strips—just trash, broken glass and gravel. The street was a series of potholes and hadn't been paved in years. So it made my heart leap a little when at 7 p.m. Elder Alvarado slapped me on the back and said, "Let's go, Elder Daybell. We're going tracting!"

It was dark outside, and all of the street lights had either burned out or had been shot out, but Elder Alvarado boldly marched us down the street. Nearly every house had people sitting on the porch who would shout something mean or vulgar, but Elder Alvarado would just smile at them and then give me a wink.

We reached a block filled with five-story apartment buildings. In the first building we taught two first discussions and gave away three Books of Mormon. I was able to give several parts of the first discussion, some from memory. At other buildings we made five return appointments. Seemingly everyone was receptive. It was a very satisfying feeling.

We concluded our exchange the next day by traveling to the city of Elizabeth, a place that made Newark look prosperous. We visited a member lady who had five kids under age eight, and whose husband had abandoned her the previous year. They'd had a hard time finding a place to live, and this apartment barely qualified as livable.

The floor consisted of plywood, the paint was peeling everywhere, there were holes in the floor and ceiling, and the only toilet was in a closet. That was their home, on a street that matched the same description, but I noticed everyone was happy! The Spirit of the Lord was there.

I was offered one of the three chairs in the home, and a dark-haired two-year-old boy climbed up on my lap. He was filthy, but as I looked down into his eyes, I saw a great soul inside that little body. It brought me to the brink of tears to think of the trials and temptations that little boy would face, but I hoped he'd earn his eternal reward for enduring such a situation. I held him tight and silently said a prayer for him. He gave me a hug when we left. I never saw him again, but I'll never forget him.

Mistaken for Ivan Drago

During the first few months of my mission, I kept my hair fairly long compared to other missionaries. Then I got transferred to Union City, where a member owned a beauty salon. She always cut the missionaries' hair for free, and on our next P-Day we went to the salon. I settled into the chair, and without any hesitation she took a razor and went right up the back of my head. I saw a substantial chunk of hair fall to the ground beside me. Before I knew it, I had a flat-top, and the sides of my head were shaved to the skin.

"That should last you for a few weeks," she said, clearly proud of her work. I mumbled my thanks, then waited for my companion, who was getting his hair cut by another worker. When he turned and saw me, he said, "Whoa! The president might not like that."

I shrugged. "Well, there's nothing I can do about it now."

That afternoon as we walked down the bustling streets of Little Cuba in Union City, all of the kids pointed at me, shouting the same phrase, then running away. Finally we asked a grinning teenage boy sitting on a porch what they were saying.

"They're saying 'Drago,'" he said. "They think you're Ivan Drago. You know, the Russian guy who fought Rocky."

By 1987, the movie Rocky IV had made its way to Spanish TV, and these Hispanic kids thought Ivan Drago himself was walking the streets of New Jersey looking for a rematch. It was definitely a stretch of the imagination, but these kids had only seen two tall white guys with flat-tops—Drago and me. I dealt with that nickname for much of my mission.

Confiding in Someone About My Gift

Even though I didn't learn the Spanish language very quickly, I immediately felt accepted and loved by the Hispanic members. I came to realize something I had never known—many of these members regularly received dreams and visions. I had continued to hide my new visionary gift and hadn't told anyone about my Flaming Gorge experience, but these people talked about their visions openly. More importantly, their friends and family members wholeheartedly accepted the visions as being authentic and sent from heaven.

During a Sunday dinner appointment with a Peruvian family, I sat down next to the husband Rafael. He had shared in Testimony Meeting that day a vision where his great-grandpa had appeared to him while he was investigating the Church in Peru. The grandpa had told Rafael to get baptized and move to America. "So here I am," he said.

My companion was talking with the other family members, so I said to Rafael, "I have visions, too, but I don't dare tell anyone. Back in Utah they'd think I'm crazy. My bishop probably would have called you into his office to chastise you after your testimony today."

Rafael looked at me in shock. "The Mormons in Utah don't talk about these things?"

I shook my head, and Rafael responded, "That's a key reason I knew the Church is true. The First Vision, the angel Moroni, John the Baptist appearing, Peter, James and John giving the priesthood, and angels at the Kirtland Temple. It's the whole foundation of the Church!"

"Oh, they'll mention those visions as historical events during Sunday School, but it's as if the members in Utah don't believe visions can still happen now."

Rafael got kind of fired up. "What's wrong with them? The veil was very thin for Joseph Smith, and it still is for me and my family. We talk about it all the time, and our ancestors help guide us."

That conversation was a turning point for me. I began to consciously work on developing my gift. Our tracting area in Union City consisted of thousands of apartment buildings along the Hudson River, and I can testify that most of them are haunted. Maybe "haunted" is too strong of a word. Better said, the buildings are inhabited by disembodied spirits who died and don't really know where to go next, so they hang around places they lived in mortality. I could sense when there were apartments that we really needed to avoid.

Sometimes families we taught would complain about supernatural disturbances, and we would use the priesthood to cast out these disruptive spirits. But often during a missionary lesson I would sense both angels and disembodied spirits in the room, and I thought, "Hey, if these spirits want to listen in, what can it hurt?"

I sometimes saw the angels talking to them afterward. I feel there were some lessons that were more effective for those spirits than for the mortals we were teaching.

My first week in the mission field in July 1987. This was about as close to Manhattan as we could get without getting in trouble.

CHAPTER NINE

❧

Many Miracles

In January 1988, I was called to train a new missionary. His name was Elder Hepworth, and we really clicked. He was from southern Utah and as tough as nails. He'd been roping wild horses in the Utah desert just a few weeks before his mission started. I'd only been in the mission field for four months myself and hardly knew Spanish. We just worked our hearts out and trusted in the Spirit, because we didn't have much else to rely on.

A Powerful Healing

In the heart of Union City we came across one of the scariest apartment buildings I had ever seen. Graffiti was scrawled across all the hallways, and the building was trashed. We were worried about knocking on doors there, but we felt compelled to go inside. On the top floor we met a man named Carlos and his teenage daughter Lina. She told us to come back when her mother Ana was home from work.

We returned the next day, and Ana kind of freaked out when she saw us in the doorway. She told us that the week before, she'd had a vivid dream of two young men in white shirts and ties entering her family's life and helping them find "eternal truths." She invited us in, and we had a very good discussion.

Lina actually progressed faster than Ana, and she was baptized about a month later.

Lina had a major medical issue, though. Her left wrist and arm had severe nerve damage, and the muscles had been deteriorating for a few months. Her arm either hung limply at her side, or she cradled it with her right hand. Their doctor was very skeptical about ever fixing the problem, but he was willing to try surgery.

Ana's holdup on getting baptized had been tithing, because she felt she needed to save money for Lina's upcoming surgery.

We continued to teach Ana, and after one discussion, both Elder Hepworth and I felt we should give Lina a priesthood blessing. I felt he should be the one to give it.

As Elder Hepworth gave the blessing, I could tell something special was happening. We had true spiritual power resting upon us. Lina started crying before the blessing ended. She could feel a tingling sensation happening in her hand, and then it moved up her arm to her shoulder. She told us she was healed.

Elder Hepworth and I looked at each other in shock. Ana asked Lina to raise and lower her arm, which she did without any pain. We all cried with joy at the miracle we had witnessed. Ana was baptized the following week and has been a stalwart, tithe-paying member ever since.

A Series of Curious Experiences

Soon afterward, we had a series of curious experiences, starting with a man named Manuel, a middle-aged Cuban pharmacist. When we taught him about the First Vision, his eyes nearly bugged out. He excitedly told us he had a similar experience as a young boy in a Cuban forest. He saw a bright light and heard a voice telling him to follow God. He had seen spirits throughout his life, and he always felt an unusual bond with the animal kingdom, even holding and caring for big poisonous snakes in Cuba.

Manuel attended church with us, but after feeling like such an outcast his entire life, the thought of organized religion just didn't work for him. I'm grateful I got to know Manuel, though, because after meeting him, I felt a lot more normal!

The other strange experiences seemed tied to the apartment buildings themselves. In some buildings we entered, the feeling was immediately dark, and we would feel a bit depressed. I really think evil spirits had gained control of those buildings, even influencing the behavior of the people living there. These spirits seemed to gang up against us in such buildings.

The first experience occurred when we approached a row of rough-looking apartment buildings. We entered the first one, and Elder Hepworth said, "This place gives me the creeps!"

I agreed that it was even more foreboding than usual, and after tracting the top two floors, we decided to get out of there. But an older man blocked our path down the stairwell, and he demanded we identify ourselves. We explained we were missionaries from the LDS Church, and he told us to come up to his apartment.

We followed him as he hobbled back up the stairs, and it turned out to be an apartment where a lady had been rude to us when we'd knocked earlier. Well, here we were again, and she turned out to be this man's wife.

She was clearly angry to see us, and she immediately left the room when we came in. Also, the evil feeling seemed to multiply in that apartment. I looked around and there were all sorts of trinkets, voodoo dolls and burning candles. I could only pray, "Father, please protect us!"

We sat down, and the man yelled for the woman to bring us something to drink. He then told me to touch his head. I looked at his skull, then glanced over at Elder Hepworth, whose eyes were as big as saucers. This guy's skull had been cut away, and there was just a piece of skin covering a two-inch square hole in the side of his head.

I touched the skin, and the man said, "That's where Fidel Castro's buddies cut my head open and gave me a lobotomy. But that didn't stop me! Ha, ha, ha!"

Things were really getting creepy now. The wife arrived with the drinks, which looked like Sprite. We took a polite sip, then I looked in the bottom of my glass. There was some sort of powder in there!

I showed Elder Hepworth, then I jumped up and said, "Well, we've got to go. Thanks for everything!" We basically ran out the door. I glanced back at the wife, and she looked demonic. Her eyes were blazing and full of hatred, and it still gives me cold chills as I think about it.

We decided to skip the rest of that block. We crossed the street, and after tracting a couple buildings we came to a door that opened into a long, very dark hall. We walked down it about forty feet and knocked on the door at the end.

An ancient-looking man opened it, and he let us in without even asking us anything. On the couch was a girl who was probably in her 20s. We sat down, and the old guy started giving sign language to the girl. He asked us a few questions, and then he would furiously sign the answer back to the girl, who would then rapidly sign back.

It was almost comical, except she was the first person we'd seen that day who seemed to have any goodness in her. We gave them a Book of Mormon and a couple pamphlets.

We had just started to leave when a younger guy named Randy emerged from the kitchen. He spoke English, and told us he was really into religion. We soon realized that was an understatement.

Randy wanted to discuss the role that Christians would play in the coming years. We turned to Section 45 in the Doctrine & Covenants and explained that Joseph Smith had received this revelation about the future and the signs of the times. He snatched my scriptures away from me and read it rapidly. He then threw it back at me and said, "That's old news, man! Don't you have anything more specific?"

I asked what he meant, and he said that he and his friends had everything figured out, but they were now looking for a few missing pieces to the puzzle. (He had the same wild-eyed look I'd seen in the woman across the street, but I don't think Randy was possessed. He basically qualified on his own, without any demonic help.)

I tried to answer his questions, but he only got more animated and aggressive. Finally I said, "Only Heavenly Father and the Savior know the hour of the Second Coming." That got him even more upset. He shouted, "That's not true! If you're the true church, get me some names and dates about these future events! I want names!"

He was still ranting as we made our second running exit of the day. I briefly considered sending the sign-language sister missionaries to visit that girl, but I changed my mind. They'd probably run into "Ranting Randy," and that would not be a good thing.

A similar experience happened a couple of days later. We knocked on a door, and a lady answered. She seemed really polite, but as we explained about the Book of Mormon, she changed into a frightening maniac right before our eyes.

She screamed, "You are of the devil! You've added to the Bible! I'm a born-again Christian, and I condemn you!" She continued shouting for another minute before I finally said, "Okay, thanks. I guess you don't want to hear our message. Please take this free Book of Mormon and just read through it."

That sent her into another profanity-laced tirade, and she wouldn't touch the book. We just shrugged our shoulders and walked away. Outside the apartment building was a small park, and we sat down on the bench. I felt like crying, and an equally frustrated Elder Hepworth sat there and muttered, "I must be changing, because the old me would've punched her lights out!"

As I cracked up, he added, "I'm serious! I wanted to kill her!" I agreed, and suddenly we were both laughing.

Hitting an Invisible Wall

An hour later, we were walking down Broadway Avenue in Union City. As we started to cross 48th Street, it felt like I slammed into a brick wall. Some unseen power was not going to let me take another step forward. I felt a prompting to tract in an old, brown building off to the right. I tried to shake it off, but the prompting came again. Elder Hepworth looked back at me, and I tried to go forward again, but couldn't. So I said, "Why don't we tract here?"

As we climbed to the top floor, a young girl named Esther came down the stairs. When she saw us, she stopped and said, "Hello, Elders. Do you want to come visit us?"

We said yes, and she led us back to her apartment. We'd never seen this girl before, but she seemed to know all about the Church. She poured us some orange juice and gave us some cookies. After a minute of small talk I asked, "Are you a member of the church?"

She gave me a surprised look and said, "Of course! Didn't you know that?" She then explained she was living with her uncle, aunt and cousins, who were also members of the Church. I asked if they'd been to any church meetings recently, and she said, "Um, a couple of years ago."

We found out that a daughter of the family lived on the floor below, along with her husband and son. They were Jorge and Yesenia Vazquez, and their son Isaac. Jorge wasn't a member, so we arranged to visit them that evening. Yesenia was eager to get active in the Church again, and after we taught Jorge the first discussion, he seemed pretty happy. He had read the Book of Mormon before, and he said, "I think it is true."

Jorge had experienced some interesting dreams about his family's future. In one dream, Jorge was fighting off Satan's efforts to get his family. Then a light came and Satan departed. In another dream, Jorge was shown Yesenia's family on a battlefield, engaging in a battle of life and death. At first they were winning, but started to lose. Then Jorge comes onto the scene, and they win the battle.

When Jorge asked me what I thought the dreams meant, I said I felt they indicated Jorge would join the Church and lead Yesenia's family back to full activity.

A few days later we met again, and the Spirit was nearly overpowering. Toward the end of the visit, Jorge stopped the discussion and said, "I wasn't going to say anything, but I just need to tell you that there are halos around you. You are both surrounded by a giant halo!"

We couldn't see the halos, but it was a special confirmation to us and to him that what we were teaching was true.

Grandpa Keith's Visit to Me

As we walked home that night, we were on a spiritual high. It was about 9 p.m., though, and we had about a 40-block walk ahead of us. Elder Hepworth just put his head down and started walking fast, and I kept pace a few steps behind him.

Then it was as if time stopped for me, because I could sense the spirit of Grandpa Keith Daybell moving along beside me. I didn't actually see him with my natural eyes, but he was tangibly there and actually rubbed shoulders with me a time or two.

I knew instantly who he was, and I could sense his happiness at my recognition of him. I perceived he was wearing an Army uniform, probably as a way to help identify himself.

We communicated telepathically, and I was given the knowledge of how proud he was of my missionary efforts, and that he had attended our discussion that night with the Vazquez family. He said he'd been assigned to help me at key times during my mission and also later in life. I felt him place his hand on my shoulder, then he departed.

I came back to my senses, and it felt like my entire body was on fire. Grandpa had radiated a light and power that I hadn't felt since my near-death experience. His visit really strengthened me. I had been battling occasional homesickness, but it ebbed away for good after that visit.

Jorge was soon baptized, and he later served as the bishop of the Union City First Ward and helped activate Yesenia's family. He and Yesenia now live in Florida and continue to make a huge spiritual impact on their family and friends.

Esther became very active in the Church, married a returned missionary, and is raising a beautiful family. I know it was the Lord's hand (or maybe Grandpa pushing against me) that stopped me from crossing the street and leading us to meet Esther that day.

A recent photo of Yesenia and Jorge Vasquez. They have been so valiant and have blessed so many lives since Jorge joined the Church in 1988.

Union City, New Jersey is in the foreground along the Hudson River, with the Empire State Building serving as a constant landmark. These are the apartment buildings where I had a steady stream of curious experiences.

CHAPTER TEN

The Concrete Jungle

In the summer of 1988, I was transferred to serve as the District Leader in downtown Newark. We had limited success there, but it was a time of personal growth. Interestingly, Newark was the one place in my mission where I didn't really have supernatural experiences. The mortals I encountered were wicked enough to keep my attention focused on personal safety and just getting through the day.

When you constantly hear sirens and get called vulgar names from every porch, you grow a little numb to your surroundings. Walking past an abandoned burning car or seeing a store window get shattered shouldn't become routine.

One day I watched out of the corner of my eye as a man pulled out a pistol, leaned across a car hood and pointed it right at me. I turned to look at him, and he suddenly started running frantically down the street. I would love to know what spooked him so badly. There's no doubt we were receiving plenty of heavenly protection.

We traveled by bus to most of our teaching appointments. After one lesson we had to switch buses at the intersection of Broad and Market Streets, the main intersection in Newark. A street preacher was there in a dark suit and top hat, shouting all

This car was down the street from our Newark apartment. It burned without interruption for several hours one day until a rain storm put out the fire.

kinds of Biblical nonsense. As he shouted, he would pace 20 yards in one direction, then abruptly turn around and pace to the exact spot he had started. The dozens of other people at the bus stop just stayed out of his way and ignored him.

Then he spotted me. He snapped out of his trance and moved in my direction. (These guys never seemed to go after my companions. It must have been the Drago effect.) I turned my back on him, but he stood directly behind me. He was my height, and I could feel his breath on my neck.

He shouted, "Some of us worship God in the right way! But there are others who worship God in the wrong way. They pollute and defile our streets with their presence!"

At that point I turned around to face him as my companion slowly backed away. The preacher continued to rant against the "white boy" who didn't belong there. His eyes were devoid of light, like I was looking into the soul of a demon.

The preacher was winning the support of the crowd, who

had tightened in a circle around us. I just kept staring into those eyes, worried if I showed any weakness the fired-up crowd might pounce on me.

The preacher's voice was rising higher, and his Biblical denunciations of me were getting more vulgar and personal. Thankfully our bus pulled up at that moment. I saw my companion get on board, then I quickly bolted through the crowd to join him. I heard the crowd mock me, but I was just happy to escape safely.

More Divine Intervention

After three exciting months living in the circus called Newark, I returned to Paterson to serve as a Zone Leader with Elder Cobb. The previous companionship had felt guided to an area of the city where there weren't a lot of Spanish-speaking people, so one afternoon we drove back into that same neighborhood. After we crossed an intersection, I heard a male voice shout, "Stop the car!"

Elder Cobb was driving, and I instinctively braced myself and closed my eyes for an impact. After a second I turned to Elder Cobb and asked, "Why aren't you stopping?"

"What are you talking about?" he asked, looking puzzled.

"You really didn't hear that?" I asked, but he shook his head.

I tried to explain before finally saying, "We must need to find somebody around here."

We parked the car and started walking down the street. I spotted a guy on a ladder painting the second story of a house and shouted up to him, "Do you know where any Spanish-speaking people live on this block?"

He pointed diagonally across the street and said, "Try that house over there." We went to the house he pointed to, and a cheerful-looking man named Rodolfo opened the door as we approached. He was just leaving, but we gave him a Book of Mormon and he said he would be interested in having us come back. Our conversation with him lasted about a minute.

I turned around to thank the guy on the ladder, but there was no sign of him. I couldn't believe it. He could hardly have climbed down to the ground in the time we had our backs to him, much less haul away the paint can and the ladder. The combination of the shouting voice in the car and the disappearing painter all within five minutes hinted that there might be something special about this family.

Rodolfo's family did join the Church within a month. We soon met the husband's sisters, Jenny and Karina. They were soon baptized as well and have been ambassadors of the gospel throughout their lives.

Victoria's Preparatory Dream

Toward the end of my mission I asked President Workman to send me deep into Jersey City with a new missionary. I wanted to have a few more miraculous experiences before I went home.

President Workman granted my wish, and I got to train Elder Maddock in a part of Jersey City that hadn't been tracted before. On our first morning together, Elder Maddock offered a most sincere and humble prayer, asking that we would be guided to someone who was seeking the gospel light.

We arose from the floor knowing that the Lord would be with us. As he prayed, I felt the name "New York Avenue" come into my mind.

Almost as if to discourage us, a fierce, cold wind started blowing, but we finally arrived at New York Avenue, which consisted of the usual row of run-down buildings. We walked down the street, but after a minute I felt we'd gone too far. We turned around and started knocking on doors in the closest apartment building.

After a few rejections, a woman opened the door. She looked at us as if we were ghosts. She then beckoned us into the apartment. Her name was Victoria, and we taught her the first discussion. We left her a Book of Mormon and a pamphlet about Joseph Smith. We agreed to return the next day.

When we came back, she had read the pamphlet and all the way to First Nephi 20. We taught her the second discussion and committed her to be baptized.

Following the discussion, she started crying and told us a special story that made me realize how closely the Lord is really watching his missionaries. Victoria had been feeling tired and depressed the day before, so she took a nap.

During this nap, she had a dream in which two young Americans in suits knocked on her door with something very important to tell her. The dream woke her up, and it seemed so vivid and lifelike that she rushed to check the door. No one was there, but she stayed awake, watching TV. About fifteen minutes later, she heard our knock.

"I was so surprised to see you at the door, but I knew you had come to see me," Victoria said. "My heart burned when I saw you."

She added that she'd been sleeping in the back bedroom with the door closed, and she never would have heard our knock if she hadn't been awakened by the dream.

She had the dream at the same time we first walked past her building. It took us about fifteen minutes to turn around, try a few other apartments, then knock on her door. It was a humbling experience to hear her story.

It was just another testimony that the Lord will send preparatory dreams to people who are ready for the gospel, just as had happened with Ana Jimenez, Jorge Vazquez, and several others.

Mad Max

Victoria was baptized two weeks later, and the ward members rallied around her. She brought several other friends to a knowledge of the gospel, including the family she worked for as a nanny. It turned out that their mother Marta had listened to the discussions in Honduras, but was never baptized because she wouldn't give up coffee. We taught them the first three discussions, and things were going well.

The only problem was that Marta's husband Max was a true Dr. Jekyll & Mr. Hyde kind of guy. He treated us great during our visits, but he was physically violent with the family after we left.

He wasn't happy Victoria got baptized, and he soon objected to his family listening to us. After another violent encounter, Marta called the police, and Max ended up in jail for a few days.

Victoria quit working for them after she learned Max wanted to kill me and was claiming I had ruined his life. She warned me Max had a big kitchen knife he was going to stab me with after he got out of jail. That made me nervous. This whole situation was getting more complicated than a Spanish soap opera!

It all came to a head about a week later. Marta tipped us off that Max was now angry at Victoria too, and he was going to come looking for her on Sunday at the church building. We alerted the bishopric, and before church they were waiting in the foyer for any sign of danger.

A member dropped Victoria off in front of the church, and she hurried inside because she'd seen Max waiting at the corner. Despite his threats against me, I felt I should try to stop him from making a scene.

I met him halfway down the block, with two members of the Elders Quorum behind me. He gave me a shove and kept walking toward the building. I told him, "If you go into the church, you'll be arrested." (I doubt too many missionaries have said that sentence to a non-member.)

"I just want to talk peacefully with Victoria," he said. "Then I'll leave."

I didn't believe him for a moment. When he got inside the foyer, he spotted Victoria and moved quickly toward her, but the bishopric was waiting for him. I was quite proud of them as they tag-teamed him to the ground then dragged him into the bishop's office.

Someone had already called the police, and they arrived in about three minutes. The police searched Max and found my favorite knife tucked into his jacket. They handcuffed him and hauled him off to jail.

This little episode occurred just as everyone was arriving for Sacrament Meeting. The two extra police cars screeching to a halt at the front doors really had everyone pumped up. There was even a small cheer when Bishop Concepcion came out of his office with a big grin, pumping his fists above his head in celebration and giving high-fives as they put Max in a squad car. The incident sure energized the congregation, and all the meetings were abuzz about it.

I felt a little depressed, though, since I'd basically sent a man to jail. But as I looked at Victoria, I realized this was the Lord's will. She glowed with happiness, and her whole countenance had changed in the past month. I know the Lord guided us to her, and I believe we were also meant to help Marta and the children escape an abusive situation.

We soon heard that Max was facing six years in prison for all of the trouble he'd been causing. The police said they expected I would have to testify against him, but Max finally used his brain. He hired a bail bondsman to get him out of jail, then he headed straight to the Newark Airport and caught the next flight to Honduras. Everyone was happy to hear that news.

Time to Get Home to Utah

In the 1980s it was somewhat of a badge of honor to extend

your mission by a month. It was a sign to everyone at home of what a righteous servant you'd been.

I could have easily extended my mission by a month and still arrived home in time to start at BYU that fall, but I'd received a very strong impression to not extend my mission beyond my July 5th release date.

On the night of July 4th the entire Spanish zone gathered on the banks of the Hudson River to watch the spectacular fireworks show, The next morning my parents arrived in New Jersey, and we met with the Workmans and the other departing missionaries for an emotional farewell testimony meeting.

My parents and I then went on a week-long tour of the Eastern States, including the Church sites in upper New York. It was wonderful to stand in the Sacred Grove and think back on that day early in my mission when the Lord had strengthened me with a glimpse of the First Vision.

We later attended the Washington D.C. Temple with Ana Jimenez as she received her temple endowment. We concluded the trip with a visit to Manhattan and the Twin Towers, along with a New York Yankees game.

We returned to New Jersey for several farewell parties. I felt so grateful for the outpouring of love I received from the members. There are so many wonderful people who helped me during my mission, but I just don't have room to mention them all in this book.

The final party was in Paterson, hosted by Jenny and Karina's family, who we had met thanks to the disappearing painter.

Jenny asked me for a priesthood blessing before I departed, and I was honored she asked me. When I ended the blessing, Jenny turned around and told me that during the blessing she had received a vision in her mind of a girl with short blonde hair praying at the side of her bed.

The girl was asking Heavenly Father to guide her and help her find the right person to spend her life with. Jenny said she felt this was the girl I would marry. I had no idea who she could be talking about. I was curious that Jenny had seen this vision of my future wife, because my plans were to return to BYU, earn a bachelor's degree, then get a master's degree in something like Ancient Scripture before teaching at an LDS institute somewhere.

I figured marriage would happen somewhere along the line, but I'd always kept in mind that my patriarchal blessing said I would marry a very special woman "at the proper time." I had always figured it would be at least a couple of years after my mission before I would meet her.

A couple of years? How about a couple of weeks.

CHAPTER ELEVEN

❖

A Quick Courtship

A week later I was home in Springville and saw my brother Paul's 1988 high school yearbook on his shelf. I flipped through it and saw a half-page feature with photos about a girl named Tammy Douglas. When I saw her face, I felt the most electrifying shock of my life. Staring back at me was a beautiful girl with short blonde hair.

I quickly turned to her senior class photo, and I was fascinated. I realized she would have been a sophomore when I was a senior, but I couldn't remember her. She would have graduated the previous year and had probably gone off to college somewhere. What were the odds I would locate her?

Thankfully, it didn't turn out to be too hard. I asked Paul if he knew anything about her, and he said, "Yeah, she's the city's cemetery secretary."

I still couldn't figure out why I couldn't remember her. Then I came to understand that some sort of spiritual veil had been placed over my mind concerning her during high school. If we had gotten to know each other at that time, we would have become inseparable. However, we still had many growing experiences to go through on our own before we became a couple. The timing wasn't right in high school for either of us.

Tammy's senior class photo, which forever changed my life for the better after I saw it in my brother's yearbook.

I later found out that Tammy had been keeping an eye on me since her sophomore year when I was on the Student Council. She had been in the audience during those crazy assemblies we did, and she admired me from afar in the school halls. While I was on my mission, she had even told her friends, "I'm going to date Chad Daybell when he gets home."

So although I didn't know it yet, things were lining up nicely in my favor.

A Wonderful Week

During my final interview with President Workman, I explained that I wanted to teach at the Missionary Training Center in Provo. I would be attending BYU, and I thought a job there would work out well. President Workman had strong connections at the MTC, and he wrote a wonderful letter of recommendation for me.

A few days after I got home I took the letter to the MTC and was interviewed on the spot. The interview went great. I filled out some paperwork and then returned the following week to teach classes to actual missionaries. An evaluator observed me, and afterward he said he was impressed. He said I should expect a call to start working there within a week. I was excited that everything had gone so smoothly.

I gave my mission homecoming talk the first Sunday I was home, but the second week I attended the Springville Singles Ward in hopes of seeing Tammy. Our eyes locked briefly when I accidentally walked into the Relief Society room, but I didn't get a chance to talk to her.

The bishopric had announced a Singles Ward Family Night for the next day, and I was really hoping Tammy would be there. When I arrived, the group was already playing a rag-tag game of volleyball. I had spotted Tammy from the moment I entered the cultural hall. She later told me she was watching me, too, although at the time I wasn't aware she knew who I was. She was on one volleyball team, so I joined the other team, and soon we rotated to be across the net from each other. We stared at each other for a moment before she confidently said, "I'm going to spike it in your face."

I smiled at her comment, but the only reply I could come up with was, "Oh yeah?"

Then the ball was served into the net and we rotated away from each other. We didn't speak again the rest of the night, although we still played a cat-and-mouse game of keeping an eye on each other.

Toward the end of the night, Les Chappell told me he wanted to go on a double-date that Friday, so I said I'd ask Tammy. I went home and called her, and I was relieved when she accepted. I later found out that Tammy had actually danced around the living room after she hung up the phone. Tammy hadn't been too big on dating, so her parents sensed from her excited reaction that she might be interested in me.

Friday finally arrived. We were both a little nervous, but I was smitten right from the start. The date went great, and we went to a fireside together at the Marriott Center two days later.

Heavenly Mischief at the MTC

That next week I returned to the MTC, because I hadn't heard anything about my job. I talked to the secretary and explained I'd gone through the whole process and was waiting to find out my starting date. "I remember you," she said. "The evaluator said you did well. Let me get your file."

She opened the filing cabinet behind her and shuffled through some papers. "I know it was right here," she said.

I waited for five minutes as she checked every possible

spot the file could be, but it just wasn't there. She called in the evaluator and asked if he had taken my file.

"No," he said. "Can't you find it?"

To make a long story short, they never found it. The evaluator finally said, "I'm sorry, but you're going to have to start over. If you fill out the paperwork today, we could have you teach a class next week."

"You already saw me teach," I said. "Can't we go from that?"

"I wish, but I need a record of the missionaries' evaluations of your teaching performance, and that group left last week," he said. "Don't worry. It will go quickly."

I was a bit perturbed, but I took the paperwork with me and returned home. I called Tammy at her job and told her, "I guess I'll just do it all again."

Tammy had other ideas. As the cemetery secretary, she knew Paul was going to quit working at the cemetery to go on his mission. Tammy called the cemetery sexton, Denny Pickering, and told him Paul's brother was looking for a part-time job.

"Really?" Denny asked. "That would be great. Have him put in an application."

Tammy called me back and said, "I think I found a job for you." I was soon hired, and that's how I got into the cemetery business. In retrospect, I know there was some heavenly intervention involved in my missing MTC file, because the cemetery job was actually a better fit for me in every way. I could work longer hours at a higher hourly wage, and I could see Tammy much more often.

Tammy's secretary office was in downtown Springville, but at times she had to bring burial reports to the Evergreen Cemetery. Denny wryly told me, "Tammy used to bring those reports up here once a week. Now she seems to come every day."

Her visits usually happened to coincide with my break time, and our "cemetery courtship" allowed us to get better acquainted.

Within a month we took the bold step of actually sitting next to each other during the Singles Ward sacrament meeting—the universal sign to other ward members we were now a couple and pretty much off limits to anyone else.

I Finally Got a "Yes!"

I began praying sincerely whether Tammy was the person I should marry. One evening I was driving home over Ironton Hill after classes at BYU. I began to pray, telling Heavenly Father that even though I'd only known Tammy for about ten weeks, I had decided to propose to her. I received such a strong "Yes!" response that it brought tears to my eyes. After so many "No!" answers over the years, I had finally received my "Yes!"

I soon "unofficially" proposed to her, then on the night before Thanksgiving I knelt down before her and gave her a diamond engagement ring. She thankfully said yes, and we spent Thanksgiving Day showing the ring to our extended families.

We registered for three classes together during BYU's winter semester, and Tammy literally saved my grade in Statistics. I never would've survived that class without her.

We were married in March 1990 in the Manti Temple and just really enjoyed being newlyweds.

After we were married, the Spirit reminded me of several vivid instances when we almost became acquainted. As I mentioned, I was a senior at Springville High when Tammy was a sophomore. Before the start of the year, I was helping create student ID cards for the incoming students. My assignment was to cut out the student photos from the previous year's Junior High yearbook. I cut out Tammy's photo and froze for a second. I looked at her name and said it aloud, intending to remember it and get to know her. But the angels must have gone to work to block my memory, because I didn't ever follow through.

Strangely, though, when Tammy and I later talked about that high school year, I could remember where her locker was before she even told me. So on some subconscious level, I was aware of her.

Tammy happened to live next door to Les Chappell, but she and I still never really crossed paths. The most memorable time we almost met was when I parked my Volkswagen the wrong direction in front of his house. As I turned off the car, Tammy got into her car that was parked right in front of me. We both sat in our cars and stared at each other for a few seconds, and there was definitely a strange spark between us. I distinctly remember my heart beating faster, but then she drove away.

Once again it was as if the Spirit worked overtime to keep us apart until after my mission, because as intertwined as our lives were with dozens of mutual friends, there wasn't a logical reason we hadn't met.

The funny thing is that Les and I spent many nights at his house talking about what lay ahead for us, and my future wife was less than fifty yards away the entire time.

Living in the "The Now"

Soon after Tammy and I were married, she was promoted to a full-time secretarial position with Springville City. The city leaders realized it was time to computerize all of the old hand-written cemetery cards, as well as double-check their accuracy. It was more work than Tammy could do on a part-time basis, so they created the new position. The job came with full insurance benefits, and it was a blessing to us.

I was still on scholarship and progressing through BYU's journalism program, while still working a few hours each week at the cemetery. We suddenly felt rich! We were eating out a lot, going to concerts, buying whole boxes of Symphony candy bars at Sam's Club, and so on. Life was great!

As I worked my way toward graduation, I was just enjoying living "in the now." For once, I had put the future out of my mind. I had an adorable, loving wife, and we were having a lot of fun together.

Wonderful In-Laws

We were busy with work and school, but we visited Tammy's family often. My in-laws Ron and Phyllis Douglas have always been wonderful to me. They accepted and loved me when I worked in a cemetery, and still loved me even after I became a journalist.

I learned that Phyllis was a convert to the LDS Church. Her father Randy Cooper had actually been baptized as a boy, but he had gone inactive by the time he married Phyllis' mother Lucille.

As Phyllis and her younger sisters grew older, Lucille wanted them to attend church, and Randy suggested they attend the LDS Church. Lucille and Phyllis took the missionary lessons and were soon baptized, and the family was sealed in the Idaho Falls Temple a year later.

As a teenager Phyllis suffered a terrible illness, and at one point her spirit left her body. She was floating near the ceiling when Lucille came in to check on her. Phyllis appeared dead, but Lucille slapped her and shook her, screaming, "You're not gonna die on me!" Phyllis obediently returned to her body.

When Phyllis told me that story soon after my marriage, I thought, "Hey, here's someone who might understand me."

It was only fitting that Tammy and I had our engagement photos taken in the cemetery. Here we are being a bit playful.

Our wedding day. We were married in the Manti Temple and then held our reception at the Springville Art Museum.

CHAPTER TWELVE

✤

Wrapping up at BYU

A big part of my junior year at BYU was spent taking the classes required to become an LDS Seminary teacher. There was intense competition for the few full-time teaching slots that would open up that year.

There were 129 students in the preparatory classes, but we were told only 12 positions would open up throughout the Church in the fall of 1992. So the odds were long to begin with, but I strongly felt I'd be teaching the gospel in some capacity in the future, and this would at least provide some training.

At the end of my junior year I was assigned to teach a Seminary class for a full week at Spanish Fork Junior High. My first day went very well, and I was feeling confident. But the class's regular teacher, a gentleman in his mid-50s, seemed intent on making things difficult for me.

For example, for the opening hymn each day, he would put a cassette tape into a boom-box and play space-age synthesizer versions of the hymns, rather than have a student play the piano.

On my second day leading the music, I got a little off the synthesizer beat. Of course, the students weren't watching me anyway as they read the words out of their hymnals, but I saw the teacher glaring at me through his office window.

Although the students had been ignoring me, they all paid attention when the teacher burst out of his office, grabbed my right arm and began guiding it gracefully through the air. He told the class, "See, this is how you do it, not how Brother Daybell was doing it!"

He continued to guide my arm until the end of the song. I felt the students' respect for me slip away, and my self-esteem dropped through the floor.

I bounced back the final three days and taught a good lesson when I was observed by a BYU supervisor on the final day, but by that point I'd decided Seminary teaching wasn't for me.

I would really love to teach it now, but at age 22 I wasn't ready to devote the next 30 years of my life to the classroom. Through this experience I gained a tremendous respect for all teachers, even the one who didn't like how I led the music.

Anyway, when the letter arrived a month later saying I hadn't been selected to continue forward in the training program, it wasn't a surprise. The letter included evaluations from the students in the class, and I was relieved to see they were overwhelmingly positive. But as the door closed on one career opportunity, thankfully another one opened.

The Daily Universe

As a journalism student, I had worked as a reporter for the Daily Universe's City Desk during my junior year, covering all the smaller communities in Utah County. I came up with some creative articles, and I grew to be good friends with the City Editor, Trent Ricks.

At the end of the semester, Trent was named the newspaper's Editor in Chief for our senior year, and within a month after being turned down as a seminary teacher, Trent hired me as the Assistant City Editor for the 1991 fall semester.

As I waited for classes to start again, I completed a 12-week internship at the Springville Herald. For each week's edition I wrote at least two articles for the front page and also compiled the police report.

I also interviewed the sculptor Gary Price for an article that would run during Art City Days. He is nationally known and very busy, but he was very gracious and gave me an extensive tour of his statue garden and studio.

That summer also included the announcement I'd been hoping to postpone for another year or two. Tammy said, "I feel it's time we start our family."

"Are you sure?" I asked. "Shouldn't we wait until I have a solid job?"

"I feel our children are ready to come," she said firmly.

I knew I couldn't argue with her. I might be the one who had visions, but when the Holy Ghost spoke to Tammy, I didn't question it. We soon had a child on the way.

Life on the City Desk

I returned to BYU for my senior year and started working at the Daily Universe. The City Editor was Bill Dermody, a talented, energetic guy from Boston, and although we'd never met before, we really hit it off and had a great time. We were fortunate to have a great group of reporters on the city desk that semester. It was exciting to be on the cutting edge of the news world.

One touching experience that semester was interviewing the parents of Brian Watkins, a Utahn who had been murdered by thieves the previous year while attending the U.S. Open tennis championship in New York City. They kindly invited me into their home, and I wrote an article that shared their feelings of what they had gone through. My heart really went out to the family for the tragedy they had endured.

I did have a few humorous experiences that final semester. Bill and I were somewhat computer illiterate and nervous about jumping into the real world after college, so we decided to take a computer class. However, the only class that fit our schedule was intended for advanced engineering students.

We realized our GPAs didn't really matter anymore, so we signed up for the class. We had to design spreadsheets, set up engineering tables, and create macros and various computer shortcuts. I actually overcame a lot of my fears about computers through that class.

Toward the end of the semester, everyone had to pair up and give a presentation on something new in front of the whole class. Bill and I came up with a short, simple spreadsheet presentation that we were certain we hadn't seen before. We confidently went to the front of the classroom, where the computer monitor was projected onto a large screen.

Bill started our presentation in his cocky Bostonian way. His confidence began to waver, though, as guys started calling out, "Hey, didn't we learn this in class the first week?" and "Come on, you're kidding me, right?"

Bill finally stopped and shouted, "We're just journalists, okay? We don't know what we're doing!"

I laughed at his comment, but no one else did. Then Bill smiled at me and said, "It's your turn," before fleeing back to his seat. I was speechless in front of that silent group. I fumbled my way through a couple of computer functions before messing them up, then I just returned to my seat. We usually applauded our classmates after a presentation, but the room was silent.

Yet both Bill and I felt giddy and euphoric! Never had we completely bombed something so horrendously in our entire lives! We laughed all day long back at the Daily Universe office.

The biggest surprise was when the presentation grades came

out. The presentation was worth 50 points, and not surprisingly, we had the lowest scores in the class. But maybe Bill's "journalist" comment gained us compassion from the instructor. Somehow Bill got a 26, and I got a 24. I would've given myself maybe four points.

The instructor, who was a great guy and the most "human" engineer I've ever met, later admitted to us that everybody got 20 points for even standing up there. So I really did only earn four points!

I studied hard on the other sections of the course, and while I was an idiot in the eyes of those engineers, I did my best. I ended up with a B- in that class, my lowest grade ever at BYU, but I'm proud of it, because I earned every bit of it.

Hoop Stars

That semester the male members of the Daily Universe staff formed an intramural basketball team. There were seven of us, and we weren't very good, but we usually kept the game close until halftime. This was mainly because the other team's players recognized our names from the newspaper. Trent would usually say something like, "You better treat us right, or your names are going to show up in the police report tomorrow."

The other team would play a bit timidly at first, but once they realized we were just a bunch of out-of-shape goofballs, we'd get stomped. Thankfully, we didn't take it seriously. Our main goal was to let everyone on the team score and to leave a few bruises on our opponents.

A highlight of my BYU experience was becoming good friends with an energetic student reporter named Tad Walch. We assigned him to cover the Provo City police beat, and he did a great job, scooping the Provo Daily Herald a few times.

It has been fun to watch Tad ascend to the pinnacle of the

newspaper industry. He currently works for the Deseret News and typically covers key LDS Church events.

Tad and I have crossed paths several times the past few years, and it's always a happy reunion. I actually named a key character in my *Standing in Holy Places* series after him. The real Tad has lived a much better life than the fictional one.

Off to New Adventures

I graduated with a bachelor's degree from BYU in April 1992. College was a stressful yet satisfying experience for me. I learned how to work well with people and became a better writer and editor. Despite my unusual career path, having a college degree has opened up many opportunities that wouldn't have come otherwise.

As I walked across the stage and received my diploma, Tammy was due to give birth in a month. I had interviewed with a few companies, but I hadn't locked down a job yet. I was worried how everything was going to work out.

Tammy was calm, though. She told me she had prayed about it and was going to quit her job when the baby was born. She was confident I would find a job to support the family. I should have trusted her. She was right all along.

Our first child Garth soon arrived, and we loved our new little son. I accepted a job at the Ogden Standard-Examiner a couple of weeks later, and we moved to Weber County to start a new adventure.

My dad getting his finger stuck while helping fix my car during the early 1990s. This photo shows why I keep my hair short now. After this hairstyle, my hair never really recovered.

Tammy and I (and Garth in her tummy) on the day of my BYU graduation in 1992.

Above: Soon after Garth was born, we visited with Les Chappell and his son Jeff. Yes, the boys' mothers were nearby to help these new fathers out.

Below: When I was the Daily Universe's City Editor, I would write regular columns, and this caricature by the staff cartoonist served as my byline.

CHAPTER THIRTEEN

The Move to Ogden

Going from BYU's Daily Universe to the Ogden Standard-Examiner was a major step up. The company was a full-scale operation with a bustling newsroom and dozens of employees, and I was right on the front lines in producing the newspaper each day.

I was hired as a copy editor, and I'm grateful the newspaper's copy chief Peggy Barney took a chance on the rookie from BYU. I bonded with some of the best co-workers I've ever had. Our staff included non-Mormons, ex-Mormons, lapsed Mormons, and a couple of active Mormons, and we all got along well.

This was an exciting time when computer typesetting programs were being introduced, but when I first started working there we still actually cut and pasted the newspaper together. On the Copy Desk we would design the pages, edit the stories, write the headlines, then send the articles to the back room. If the article ended up being longer than we planned, I would go to the back room and decide which part of the story to cut out. Then with a knife we would literally cut the text and paste it onto the page board. Then I would check the entire page and sign off on it. If there was an error, it was my fault.

So there was a lot of stress as the daily deadline approached, with people running everywhere and shouting to each other as we all tried to do three things at once. I would be editing a last-minute article but listening for someone to shout, "Chad, get back here and cut this story!" or "That headline isn't long enough. Rewrite it!"

The job was invigorating, and although I wasn't earning a master's degree as I had once planned, I was experiencing a hands-on crash course in writing, editing, and publishing. That's why my novels feel like an all-knowing reporter is describing the action. Some people would like me to write flowing, poetic verse with lots of adjectives and adverbs, but that's just not my style. I was trained as an editor to chop out the excess and get right to the point.

Randy Hollis was the sports editor. He had written and published a book, and I was impressed. Tammy and I would go to the Weber County Library, and I imagined what it would be like to see my name on the spine of a book there. But the editing job kind of fried my brain each day. After eight hours on the computer at work, the last thing I wanted to do was go home and type. Besides, I had no idea what to write about, so I put the idea on the back burner.

The eight-hour shifts went quickly, because you really didn't have a break. On Friday and Saturday nights, it was usually just one other copy editor and myself designing each page and writing every headline in the newspaper.

Since I had an interest in sports, I became the main copy editor for the sports section, and I really enjoyed that. Friday nights during football season were always a mad scramble as the high school football stories came rolling in all at once. Then we'd get to do it all again the next night with the college football games. Somehow by 12:15 a.m. we had put the newspaper together and sent it to press.

Despite the excitement of the job, it was physically wearing me down. At that time the Standard-Examiner was an afternoon paper, with morning deliveries on Saturday and Sunday. So I would work on Tuesday, Wednesday, and Thursday from 4:30 a.m. to 1 p.m., then reverse the clock on Friday and Saturday and work from 4 p.m. to 12:30 a.m. I got Sundays and Mondays off.

The schedule was really nice in terms of being with Tammy and our young children for most of the day, but I rarely got a good night's sleep because of getting up so early and then switching the schedule on the weekends. Plus, I was getting paid what copy editors usually earned—not a whole lot.

We first lived in a one-bedroom apartment in Layton, and it was cramped. One day I was doing the final proofreading of the sports section, and I felt prompted to read the want ads as well.

A certain ad for a two-bedroom apartment in the nearby community of Washington Terrace seemed to jump off the page at me. I called the number right away, and the landlord was shocked to receive my call.

"I just called in that ad this morning," he said. "How did you see it already?"

I smiled to myself and said, "Well, I read it in the newspaper."

He showed us the apartment that afternoon and we signed the lease right then. It cut down my daily commute by about 20 minutes each way, and it turned out to be a great place for us.

Tom's Tragic Fall

The assistant news editor, Tom Christensen, really helped me during the first few months on the job. He was also a BYU graduate and was active in the Church. Tom and I usually arrived at the same time in the morning and got things underway on the copy desk.

One morning in January 1993 I got to work, but there was

no sign of Tom. There had been a major snow storm the night before, and I figured it was just taking him longer than usual to get to work.

An hour later, our boss Peggy got a call from Tom's wife Christine telling her Tom wouldn't be able to come to work because he'd suffered a terrible injury.

We learned later in the day that Tom had tried to remove a large build-up of snow on his roof before coming to work and fell off in the process and broke his back. He was paralyzed from the waist down, and was hospitalized for several months. It really put my own life in perspective. It was sobering to see how quickly life can change.

Six months later, he wheeled back into work to the cheers of his co-workers. It was great to have him back. He and I would often eat lunch together and discuss the BYU Cougars.

We stayed in touch through the years, and I visited him in the Standard-Examiner newsroom a few times when I was passing through Ogden. Tom had called me in early 2014 about possibly doing a book together about the struggles he had endured, and he seemed in good spirits.

So it was a shock a few months later when Peggy posted on Facebook that Tom had passed away. He was in a wheelchair for the last two decades of his life, but he never lost his sense of humor in spite of many health problems.

Much like Milt Harrison from my youth who endured physical setbacks with grace and humor, Tom Christensen is one of my true heroes.

An Unusual Book

As I mentioned earlier, my mother-in-law Phyllis and her family had joined the LDS Church when she was young. They'd discovered some of Lucille's family history through the years, but there weren't a lot of family records to work from. The temple work had been done for only a few of the ancestors on that side of the family.

I had taken a Family History course at BYU, and Tammy and I had made some exciting finds at the Church Family History Center in Salt Lake. We were able to do the temple work for nearly 100 people, but then we were stumped again.

When I took the job at the Ogden Standard-Examiner, I discovered there was a small Family History library just a few blocks away. I visited it one day after work and browsed the shelves. Suddenly the spine of a small volume wedged between two thick books seemed to "supersize" for a few seconds, then it went back to normal. That caught my attention.

I pulled it off the shelf and read the title: *Osborne County, Kansas Cemeteries*. I opened it and was surprised to see the names and death dates of people Tammy and I had discovered in the U.S. census records the previous year. These ancestors were buried in this rural Kansas county I had never heard of. I made photocopies of several of the pages and took them home to Tammy. We began working on those family lines.

I have thought often about that small volume, because I don't think it was even in the right section of the library. If the title on the spine hadn't miraculously tripled in size right before my eyes, I never would have noticed it.

That little book opened the way for us to obtain a much larger book about Osborne County filled with names, birth dates, and family relationships. We did the temple work for hundreds of those ancestors throughout the 1990s.

Above: Tammy and Garth at a wedding reception. They are both adorable!

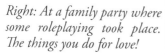

Right: At a family party where some roleplaying took place. The things you do for love!

CHAPTER FOURTEEN

---- ⚜ ----

My Second Near-Death Experience

In 1993 my wife Tammy and I went on a family vacation to San Diego, California with my parents and siblings. We always visited La Jolla Cove during our vacations, and on this particular day we put on our swimsuits and got ready to go. Our oldest son Garth was just a year old, and it was overcast and a bit windy, so Tammy decided to stay at the hotel and swim in the pool with him.

I traveled with my parents and siblings to the cove. We found some shells on the beach, but there was a neat rock formation nearby that had been exposed by the low tide. My brother Brad and I climbed out onto the rocks. They seemed to get more jagged and sharp the farther we went out into the water, and the waves started to come in more forcefully. Brad decided to go back to the beach, while I stayed out on these rocks looking for neat seashells to take to Garth.

Suddenly I looked up and there was a monstrous wave bearing down on me. My dad was watching me from the beach, and he estimated it was at least 15-feet high. I was in a precarious position on the tip of the rock outcropping. For a split second

I considered trying to ride the wave in, but I would have surely been sliced apart by the jagged rocks.

An audible voice shouted in my ear, "Get down and cling to that rock." I did as the voice commanded and grabbed hold of a two-foot-wide boulder just as the wave crashed down on me. The force was incredible, and it took all of my strength to not get ripped away and tossed around.

Then my surroundings changed and I found myself in the proverbial tunnel of light. It wasn't a bright white light, but more like a yellow heat lamp. It felt like I was wrapped in a warm blanket or a cocoon, and I felt extremely happy.

I saw two male figures standing about ten feet above me. I'm certain one of them was my Grandpa Keith, while I believe the other one was Finity Daybell.

I was completely out of my body, standing in front of them. Keith was speaking to me and gesturing with his hands. He mentioned my children and described the roles they would play in the future. He also explained the tasks I needed to accomplish.

Finity didn't speak, but he watched me intently. Finally Keith asked if I would be willing to fulfill the assignments he had outlined, and I agreed to do so. Then he made a motion with his hand, and I was suddenly back in my body, which had washed closer to shore. I felt like I was wrapped in a soft, protective heavenly cushion as another wave propelled me over the rocks and onto the beach. I credit this cushion for helping me escape additional serious injuries.

Dad and my brothers were rushing toward me. Dad said, "When I saw that wave headed toward you, I could only turn my back, expecting the worst. I was sure you were dead."

I guess he was half-right.

We looked at my hands, and my fingertips were all shredded from where I had clung to the rock. The left side of my back had large bloody gashes, which must have happened while I was out of my body. My brothers helped me to the van, where a lifeguard stopped to check on me. He angrily said, "Didn't you see the sign to stay out of there? A guy died there yesterday!"

I just shook my head and said, "Sorry, I didn't see the sign."

We loaded me up and took me to the hospital to get examined. I didn't have any broken bones, but I got a lot of stitches!

Unlike other near-death experiences, I wasn't taken to a glorious city or given a tour of the Spirit World. It was more like an urgent business meeting where Grandpa Keith poured information into me during the minute or so I was out of my body.

There was also a long-term effect from the incident. My personal veil had been ripped open even wider, and this time it didn't close up nearly as much as it had after my Flaming Gorge experience.

I could remember Keith speaking with me, but the actual conversation about my future tasks was removed from my mind. I just knew it had to do with the future earthly missions of my children—four of whom hadn't been born yet.

I started having deja vu experiences, along with waking visions of future events happening in certain locations. I also began having direct intervention in my life from the other side.

A Strong "No" on Getting a Masters Degree

The first example of this newfound intervention came not long after I returned to Ogden after the vacation. During the trip, Dad had strongly encouraged me to start working on a master's degree through Utah State. It made sense if I wanted to move up in the publishing world.

I went to the Utah State University extension office in downtown Ogden and picked up an application. But as I sat down at a table and started filling it out, it felt like the pen I was holding was on fire. I dropped it, and I distinctly heard the words, "Stop! This is the wrong direction for you. You won't need additional schooling to accomplish your life's mission."

The voice was accompanied by one of the strongest "burning of the bosom" moments I've ever had. I stood up and threw the application in a recycling bin. This answer really was a shock to me, because my long-term goal growing up had been to eventually earn a doctorate degree.

The interesting thing is that although I was the most studious of my brothers, they all now have advanced degrees and I don't. But the voice was correct. If I had returned to college, none of what has happened in my career would have taken place. I never would have become an author or been in a position to form a publishing company.

Emma Appears to Me

Tammy became pregnant that summer with our second child. I was feeling a lot of pressure at the newspaper, and the answer to not get a master's degree left me feeling stuck in a professional rut that I couldn't escape from.

I went to the Ogden Temple to do some work for Tammy's ancestors, then I stayed in the Celestial Room quite a while, sitting in a chair away from everyone else. As I was praying, I felt a magnificent presence next to me.

I looked up and saw a beautiful woman with shoulder-length dark hair standing a few inches off the ground, and she had placed her right hand on my back.

I knew instinctively that this was Emma, the daughter whose physical body was currently developing inside Tammy. A comforting feeling passed through me, and she assured me everything would work out. Then she was gone, but a great feeling of love passed over me, and I knew that she was a special girl who would bless many lives.

A Vision of All of My Children

The visit from Emma was comforting to us, but the thought of another child was somewhat daunting. Despite Tammy's best efforts, Garth was turning into a wild child. He would get into the kitchen cupboards and dump everything out, particularly syrup.

He was also a master climber. If he saw Tammy put cookies in the cupboard above the fridge, he'd find a way to get them when she wasn't looking. He was too cunning for a one-year-old, and it was getting very frustrating.

On my next visit to the Ogden Temple I again prayed and contemplated my family's future. I was blessed to receive a special vision where I was shown our children many years down the road. The kids seemed to be in their early 20s to late teens, and they were wearing Church clothes. It seemed to be a special event.

I watched them interact with each other from about 10 feet away. I recognized Garth, and he still had lighter hair. He was talking to a taller young man with brown hair.

There were also two girls in the dream. The older one had dark short hair, and she was smiling at a girl with blonde hair. The four kids talked among themselves for a moment, then a brown-haired boy in his early teens came skipping into the room saying, "Don't forget about me! Don't forget about me!"

He joined the four others and smiled in my direction. This boy was the exact image of our son Mark, right down to the mischievous smile. I knew I was seeing the five children that Tammy and I would raise. It was neat to see their hair color and even their personalities.

I went home and told Tammy about the vision. It brought us great peace of mind to know that Garth might someday behave!

A Move to Downtown Ogden

One day we received notice that our landlord was going to raise our rent by $75. That seemed like an enormous amount to us at the time. We loved our nice apartment in a calm part of Washington Terrace, and we had many reasons to just tighten the budget a little more and stay there. But we felt prompted to start looking for a house. I had just received my first raise to $10.50 an hour, and about the only place in Utah you could buy a house on that salary was downtown Ogden.

We looked around and were frustrated at the lack of available quality homes, but then one came together for us. It was on 30th Street and would cost $48,000. The monthly payment would be almost exactly what our rent would be if we stayed in Washington Terrace. An older widow lived there, and she had taken decent care of it. It had a nice backyard, a one-car garage, and a basement.

The next 10 months were a little scary and frustrating at times. The house had several problems we had overlooked during the purchasing period, such as no shower. Also, when it rained hard, water would literally run through the basement.

It was a rough neighborhood at night, and I hated leaving my family alone on the weekends when I went to work. On the plus side, all of our neighbors were also poor, so we fit right in.

Not long after that, we received a shock—Tammy was pregnant again. Emma was barely nine months old, and so we would have three children under four years of age. It threw us for a loop for a few days, but in reality the recent vision I'd had of our children was a comfort. I had also been having dreams about a little boy with crazy brown hair, clear blue eyes, and a big smile. We quickly became excited about this new baby who would be coming to our family.

We decided his name would be Seth, and when he was born we had a curious occurrence. Within seconds of his birth, the nurse handed him to Tammy, and Seth looked at both of us very seriously, as if he was checking to make sure he'd come to the right parents.

It was like looking into the eyes of an ancient soul. Then suddenly his eyes clouded up like a typical newborn. Tammy and I raised our eyebrows at each other in wonderment about this new child.

Emma Cuts Her Forehead

A few months later, little one-year-old Emma was playing in our backyard. I told her to come inside so she wouldn't get hurt, but as I turned my back on her for a brief second, she fell and hit her forehead on our back step. It left a deep cut, and we took her to the emergency room where they stitched it up.

The memorable thing is that the doctor numbed the cut with a product that apparently contained cocaine. Soon afterward, Emma was literally climbing and jumping off the couches in the waiting room. We could hardly catch her. The drug had quite an effect on her!

This accident was also the basis of what later became a key scene in my first novel, *An Errand for Emma*, where Emma hits her head on a tombstone and goes back in time.

Above: Here I am after being released from the hospital following my near-death experience. My chin and the left side of my back got a bunch of stitches, while the right side was scraped raw.

Right: Little Emma's forehead after getting her own set of stitches. Let's just say it looked a lot worse beforehand.

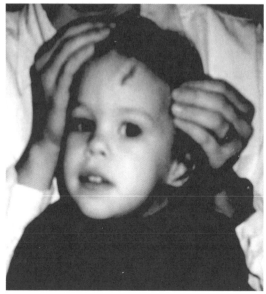

Chapter Fifteen

※

A Return to the Cemetery

After three years in Ogden, Tammy and I both felt a yearning to have our children grow up near their grandparents and cousins. Plus, the newspaper job was affecting my health. I had gained quite a bit of weight, and the relentless weekly schedule was wearing me down. We felt a change was coming in our lives.

One night my brother Paul called me to say Denny Pickering was going to retire as Springville's cemetery sexton. Paul thought I might be interested in applying, since I had cemetery knowledge and experience other candidates might not have.

It would definitely be an unusual career change, but Tammy and I felt like it was the right time to make a move. I interviewed for the position and was hired the next week. So I went from writing headlines to digging graves, but it paid better and allowed us to move back to Springville.

I stepped right into the job and really enjoyed the fresh air and regular hours. However, following my second near-death experience, I definitely was much more aware of the otherworldly nature of the occupation. When I worked in the cemetery in the past, I suspected that there were spirits nearby, but now I was certain there were plenty of "friends" hanging out with me.

Eddie the Lock Picker

The most tangible ghostly experience I had as sexton occurred after we buried a man named Eddie, who had been known in town as a petty thief. His burial spot wasn't far from my office, and almost immediately after his funeral weird things started happening.

When I arrived the next day, the gate was open to the enclosure where we kept the backhoe and dump truck. This was unusual, because I always checked that lock when I left in the evening. It's possible I'd accidentally left the gate open the first time, but after it happened three times that week, I strongly suspected Eddie was still picking locks despite being dead.

As I left work after the third incident, I tucked a piece of plastic around the lock in a certain way so I could tell if someone touched it. I drove to the cemetery that night at nine o'clock to check the lock. It was still fastened securely.

When I arrived early the next morning I immediately checked the gate, and the lock was undone. The plastic was still in place, but somehow the gate had been pushed open a few inches! I wasn't very amused by this ghostly prankster.

The biggest surprise came moments later when I checked the shed next to my office. The shed had a padlock that required a key, but not only was the shed unlocked, but the padlock itself was hooked on a peg above the door!

By this point I wasn't scared—I was mad. I figured Eddie was nearby, probably pleased I'd noticed his handiwork. So I turned around and said, "Hey Eddie, listen to me! I'm impressed with your skills, but you're going to get me in trouble. What if someone sees the open gate and steals the backhoe? I'd get fired."

I paused for a few seconds, then added, "Eddie, you don't belong here. There's a better place for you. Look around, go toward the light, and don't come back!"

He must have listened, because I didn't have any problems with the locks after that.

Hanging Out with My Friends

When I was alone in the cemetery office on frigid, foggy days, I often sensed otherworldly visitors accompanying me. It was on such days that I would catch up on my record-keeping, and invariably I'd soon notice the hair on the back of my neck standing on end, as if someone was leaning over my shoulder reading what I had written.

I knew my ghostly friends didn't mean me any harm, but I had to smile when I would leave the office for lunch and return to find a pen had been moved from where I'd left it. Sometimes I would arrive in the morning to find my day planner was already turned to the right day. That must have taken a lot of effort!

I generally sensed five men hanging around me. I understood they had lived in Springville many years earlier and had been friends during their mortal lives. They weren't particularly religious, and weren't too interested in moving into the light. They considered themselves guardians of the cemetery, but there were days when I just had to say, "Guys, get out of here! I'm trying to get some work done!" And they obliged.

Bad Vibes

There were some parts of the cemetery where negative feelings were very strong. I always had a strange feeling about a certain section, although there was no logical reason for it. It was as if someone was upset I was there.

I hadn't ever told anyone about it, though. Then one day our secretary brought me a burial order and said, "I hate that part of the cemetery. It gives me the creeps!"

I looked at the paper, and sure enough, the burial order

was in the exact area that gave me chills. I was surprised at her statement, and I explained to her how I felt in that spot. She grimaced and actually shivered from head to toe.

"It feels like someone is playing with my hair when I'm over there," she said. "I hate it!"

Truly Scared

There was an actual mood change in the cemetery once the sun set. I wouldn't necessarily call it sinister, but certainly it was more frightening and tense. Despite all the time I spent in the cemetery, if I had to go out there at night, I was definitely on edge. Every sound made me jump.

But my scariest experience happened in broad daylight. One woman's grave was well-known for being supposedly haunted, and I avoided it. But it so happened that a lady died and would be buried in the plot next to the haunted grave. In order to get the new burial in the right spot, I would have to use one of our metal probing rods to locate the vault of the haunted grave. I should've waited until my crew was with me, but I didn't.

I've gone over the next few seconds in my mind a thousand times, but there was no denying that when the probing rod hit the vault, a jolt of electricity shot through my body. I dropped the rod and just stood there until my arms stopped tingling. I wondered if I'd struck an underground electric wire, but it was impossible.

I grabbed the rod one more time and probed again, and this time when I touched the vault it felt like somebody shoved me viciously in the chest. I took off running as fast as I could as a demon-like spirit chased me all the way to my office. I could sense it clawing at me. Every inch of my body was covered in goose bumps, and I was praying aloud all the way.

My office was several hundred yards away, but I covered

the distance in record time. I was honestly terrified. One of my teenage workers was nearby the office and he came to my side. He said, "Man, you look pale! Are you okay?"

I nodded that I was fine, but I decided not to tell him what had happened. It was very real, though.

Anyway, we still had to dig that grave the next day. I dug the new grave as far from the haunted grave as I could. I wasn't going to risk the chance of another supernatural encounter. We didn't have any more problems. I figure I unleashed that demon, and now it was hopefully gone for good.

In contrast to that experience, one of my most memorable burials was when a neighbor lady I was close to passed away. She was a true saint, and after her graveside service the family was gone and the burial vault employee hadn't arrived yet. So it was just me—and her—at the graveside.

A warm feeling filled my heart, and I knew I was in the presence of an angel. My friend was telling me goodbye, and that she was now in a wonderful place.

Leah's Miraculous Birth

In the spring of 1997 we felt it was time to add another child to our family, but we were already bursting at the seams with three kids in the double-wide mobile home we had bought after moving from Ogden.

One particular home in Springville really stood out to us. Our only reservation was that Tammy's parents and most of her siblings lived in that ward. We worried about potentially being too close to the relatives, but we prayed about it, and it was clear we were meant to live there. It turned out to be a great experience to live in that neighborhood.

A year later, Tammy was eight months along with our fourth child, a girl we had already named Leah in honor of Milt

Harrison's wife. I got an urgent call one morning at work that Tammy's mom Phyllis was taking her to the Payson Hospital and I needed to meet them there.

When I arrived, Tammy was in a hospital gown waiting for her doctor to see her. She was lying on a bed and explained to me how she'd felt something pop deep inside her. As we talked, she suddenly started bleeding heavily, and it turned into a frantic situation. I gave her a quick priesthood blessing, then the nurses rushed her into an operating room. Phyllis and I got out of the way and then waited anxiously.

I snuck down the hall and peered through the room's small window. All I could see was the top of Tammy's head as several nurses and two doctors surrounded her. I was scared, but I also felt it wasn't Tammy's time to die.

Within a couple of minutes, Leah was born via emergency Caesarean section about four weeks early. She was very tiny, but she rebounded quickly and soon was the same size as other children her age. Needless to say, the doctor told us that Tammy was done having kids. He'd had to slice through her stomach muscles to save Leah, and combined with other factors, he advised her against ever getting pregnant again.

At the time, I was just relieved Tammy and Leah were okay, but lingering in the back of my mind was the sing-song chant of an unborn child saying, "Don't forget about me!"

Writing the Emma Trilogy

Around that time, the cemetery got hit by a big snowstorm overnight. We had a funeral coming that day, so I was shoveling a path across the grass to the gravesite. From out of nowhere came a voice that said, "It's time to write your books." This came as a complete surprise to me. I'd written some family histories and had the desire to write a novel, but I'd never been able to come up with a plot for a book. I leaned on the shovel and said aloud, "That's great, but I have no idea what to write about."

Almost immediately, the entire plot of my first novel *An Errand for Emma* came to me where a teenage girl goes back in time to 1868 to solve a family history mystery. I felt I should base the girl on my own daughter Emma.

I jotted down a short summary during my lunch break, then I worked on the book at night for the next few weeks. I submitted the manuscript to Cedar Fort Publishing, and I was offered a publishing contract.

To my surprise, the novel became a regional bestseller, and I got a lot of publicity in the newspapers about the gravedigger who wrote a book.

Cedar Fort wanted me to write a follow-up book, but I couldn't come up with a good idea. So I did the logical thing and prayed about it while I was working in the cemetery. I didn't hear a voice this time, but the plot to *Doug's Dilemma* filled my head, as well as the plot for *Escape to Zion*. These three books became known as The Emma Trilogy, a time-travel series that were based on my own children.

Doug's Dilemma is a mix of my own missionary experiences combined with Grandpa Keith's World War II dangerous exploits. It ended with a cliffhanger leading to the final book in the trilogy.

As I worked on *Escape to Zion* in 2000, I kept having a dream that the Twin Towers in New York City were burning. In the dreams I was always on the street below the towers. They were both on fire and people were running and screaming. I didn't know the cause. From my vantage point, it seemed like all of Manhattan was on fire.

This dream had deep personal significance, since I served my entire mission in New Jersey along the Hudson River. The Twin Towers were like a central beacon to me. I decided to include portions of the dream in *Escape to Zion*. In the book, the main character Emma is in the future, and she reads an old newspaper about the Twin Towers being burned. So it kind of threw me for a loop when it actually happened a year later.

The trilogy was a success with readers, and we took a few family trips around the western United States doing book signings at LDS bookstores. Tammy would take the kids to historical sites during each signing, and we had a lot of fun.

Vision of Seth Being Killed

As I worked on these novels, I began having even more dreams and visions relating to my family's future. For example, one night I had a vivid dream that Tammy had taken the kids to the Spanish Fork Kmart. In the dream, I watched Tammy lead the kids across the parking lot to the store entrance. Then little Seth broke free and stumbled ahead of the others. I distinctly noted he was wearing a particular pair of blue overalls.

Just then a blue Cadillac driven by a Polynesian man came speeding by and ran over Seth, killing him instantly. The dream obviously disturbed me, but I had to leave for work before Tammy woke up, so later that morning I called her. Before I could even tell her about the dream, she said, "I've got the kids ready and I'm taking them to Kmart."

I immediately asked what Seth was wearing, and it was the blue overalls. I told her about the dream, and we agreed I should go to the store with them. They picked me up at the cemetery, and I carried Seth into the store. Everything was exactly as I had seen in the dream in terms of the angle of the sun, and so on. We didn't see a blue Cadillac, though. I believe we altered the timeline by a few minutes when Tammy picked me up to go with them. I have no doubt it was a warning dream sent straight from heaven.

"We Hate Your Books!"

I was confident that my books were inspired from a heavenly source, and I knew that writing them was helping fulfill my promise to Grandpa Keith. But it always helps when the dark side reinforces that you are on the right track.

One night as I was falling asleep, I heard a rustling noise outside our bedroom window. As I lay there, a dozen voices suddenly shouted in unison, "We hate your books!" It was fairly loud, and I looked over at Tammy, but she was asleep.

Then they repeated the phrase. I jumped up and looked out the window, but no one was there. The voices were high-pitched and certainly not mortal. I knew I'd been visited by evil spirits.

I had used the priesthood to dedicate our home after we moved in, but now I rededicated it, along with all of our property, commanding these evil spirits to never return. I didn't have any more trouble after that.

The encounter actually strengthened me to know that the adversary wasn't pleased with the books I was writing. Their plan backfired on them, but no one has ever accused evil spirits of being too bright.

"Don't Forget About Me!"

As 1999 progressed, Tammy and I discussed whether to have a fifth child. I didn't press the issue, because the doctor had been so adamant that Tammy's life would be at risk if she became pregnant again.

But Tammy hadn't forgotten my vision of the our children either. The phrase "Don't forget about me!" seemed to come up a lot in our daily lives.

We had some serious concerns after Leah's traumatic birth, but we also had faith the Lord would watch over Tammy. She became pregnant in the summer of 1999, and thankfully there were few complications. Our son Mark was born in March 2000. Thankfully, he looked like the child who had skipped into the room in my vision!

It strengthened our testimony to see how each child had the hair color and other characteristics matched that vision, and we knew our family was now complete.

This photo was taken a few months after Mark was born, during one of our booksigning trips. The kids were a bit of a handful, but we had a lot of fun.

I enjoyed doing booksignings. It was a nice break from the cemetery routine.
I was grateful for the warm reception my novel received.

BOOKMARK TOP 10 SELLING BOOKS

#1	"Errand for Emma"	Chad Daybell
#2	"For Love Alone"	Anita Stansfield
#3	"Sunshine for the LDS Soul	Various Authors
#4	"Rumors of War"	Dean Hughes
#5	"Strengthening Marriage"	Doug Brinley
#6	"Ariana"	Rachel Nunes
#7	You Are Special"	Max Lucado
#8	"Work & Glory vol. 9"	Gerald Lund
#9	"Far from Home"	Dean Hughes
#10	"Zion, Seeking the City of Enoch"	Larry Barkdull

Chapter Sixteen

Choosing Between Two Paths

I was really enjoying the success of the Emma Trilogy, but I still had to work most Saturdays at the cemetery. It was hard to schedule a book signing when there was a pretty good chance I would need to do a burial that day. I needed a good 9 to 5 job that would free up my weekends.

My brother Matt had been working for a company in Colorado called Access Computer Products while he was attending Colorado State University. The company president wanted to expand their Utah operations and was looking for a full-time person to run an office in Provo.

Matt told me it would be a great opportunity. I looked into it, and I saw how it could work out well. I would make as much money as I earned at the cemetery, with the potential to make a lot more.

Once Mark was born, I felt I could take the leap. I resigned as the Springville cemetery sexton and became the Utah area manager for Access. I started with a few small sales accounts that quickly blossomed. We specialized in selling laser printer cartridges, and we also partnered with elementary schools to collect used cartridges that could be remanufactured.

We carved out a niche in the market that had been untapped,

and the company grew rapidly. Within a few months we were doing so well that we added a few employees and moved the entire operation to a large warehouse in Orem. The work environment was relatively stress-free, and all aspects of my life were going smoothly.

The Emma Trilogy was selling well, and I wrote a short, humorous book about my cemetery experiences entitled *One Foot in the Grave*. Then I put my writing on the backburner while I worked to make Access Computer Products even more successful.

The Lord had other plans for me, however. One afternoon I received a call from the owner of Cedar Fort. He told me he needed a managing editor. I had done some freelance editing work for them the previous year, and they were pleased that my books were selling well. He offered me the position, saying I would be a great fit with the other employees.

I explained to him I was happy where I was working, but I was intrigued by this chance to climb the ladder in the publishing world. I asked how much he could pay me, and he gave a figure that made me involuntarily cringe. The offer was $10,000 less per year than I was already making. I had a wife and five little kids at home, and taking a pay cut like that would really tighten our budget almost to the breaking point.

I told the publisher I needed to think about it and discuss it with my wife. I called Tammy, and she had the same financial concerns I did. She suggested I call my boss in Colorado and see if there wasn't a way to somehow do both jobs. I gave him a call, and he was quiet as I explained the situation.

Then he said, "Let me make this easy for you. You've been doing a great job for us. Let's jump your salary up another $20,000 a year, and you can forget about that other place. They can find someone else."

I couldn't believe my luck. It was a pay raise beyond my

wildest dreams. I said, "That sounds great to me! Thank you so much."

I hung up the phone and started dialing my house to tell Tammy the great news, but as I did so it felt like a heavy blanket had been draped across my shoulders. It nearly knocked me off my feet. A voice said, "This is not part of your life plan. This isn't the right path."

The words felt like a punch in the face, but I knew it was true. I had known since I was in the fourth grade that I would be a writer and an editor. That's what I had been trained to become at BYU and the Ogden Standard-Examiner. The fact I was now a published author was somewhat miraculous in itself.

A Vision of Two Paths

As I pondered what the voice had told me, a vision opened up in my mind. I saw two paths ahead of me. I first followed the one on the left, which showed me staying with the computer company. My family became financially well-off, and I rose to a top management position in the company. I saw us living in a big home, but I was aware the job would eventually require a lot of travel and would affect my family.

I sensed I didn't progress too far spiritually, and neither did my family. I never had time to write additional books, and the lives of my children seemed to be hollow shells compared to what they could become.

In the vision I then retreated back to the starting point and took the path on the right. I saw financial challenges and many stressful situations, but I also saw a strong marriage and a unified family. I was shown the faces of many people I would assist in publishing their messages to the world. I sensed having great satisfaction in my work, and that this occupation would help my family stay close to the gospel.

Then the vision closed. Frankly, the extra money was still tempting, but I had gotten the message. I picked up the phone and told Tammy what had transpired. It was the hardest call I have ever made. She is a great woman of faith, though, and she felt calm about the decision to work for Cedar Fort, despite the hardships it might bring.

I called back my boss in Colorado and told him my decision. He couldn't believe it, but he was a spiritual man, and as I gave him additional details, he understood. Over the next two weeks I trained my replacement at Access Computer Products, then I began working full-time in the LDS publishing world. Taking the path on the right was difficult, but I had chosen to put God first, and it has made all the difference.

CHAPTER SEVENTEEN

❖

Joining Cedar Fort

I was signed to my first publishing contract by Cedar Fort's editor-in-chief Lee Nelson. During the 1980s and 1990s, Lee was about as famous as you could get in our little corner of Utah County. He had written the fictional *Storm Testament* series as well as the *Beyond the Veil* series, and the books had sold nearly a million copies.

Lee owned a nice home and ranch in the middle of Mapleton, and I grew up with Lee's oldest son Richard. There was always a little buzz in the crowd if Lee attended one of Richard's sporting events.

So I was a little awestruck as I began working with him. We got along well. He was a cowboy at heart, and he'd often come to the office with hay on his Wranglers from feeding the horses that morning. Lee was a wonderful mentor to me.

We worked together to jumpstart the editorial department, and then a wonderful woman named Georgia Carpenter was hired as the marketing director. She had many years of experience in the publishing industry, and suddenly we had a very strong team.

I had several non-fiction book ideas percolating in my mind, and as I presented them to our editorial board, they encouraged me to write them. Within a year I had written several bestsellers, including *The Aaronic Priesthood*, *The Youth of Zion*, and the *Tiny Talks* series for Primary children that Tammy and I wrote together.

I was doing one or two booksignings each Saturday, and Tammy even did a few signings for *Tiny Talks* at stores along the Wasatch Front. A highlight was when Deseret Book paid for us to participate in a Las Vegas booksigning event at one of the stores there. (Don't worry, we stayed away from the casinos.)

The "Made Easier" Series

Our stake president at the time was David Ridges, who was getting close to retiring from teaching at the Orem LDS Institute. We also happened to live around the corner from each other, and our families knew each other well. He even once rescued my wife and children by throwing snowballs at some vicious dogs that were chasing them.

He had published a small book on his own called *Isaiah Made Easier*, and I felt a powerful prompting to talk to him about writing more books. However, that same week he cut his hand badly while operating an electric saw in his garage, and it was clear he wasn't going to be typing again anytime soon.

A couple of months later I saw his wife Janette in the grocery store, and the Spirit commanded, "Go tell her that Dave needs to write more books."

I approached her and explained I was now the Managing Editor at Cedar Fort. I told her I felt Dave ought to write another book, and she said she'd discuss it with him.

The next Sunday after Sacrament Meeting I talked with Dave in the foyer, and he said he felt good about it. We worked out a game plan to start a "Made Easier" series that would evaluate each verse of scripture. We reissued *Isaiah Made Easier*, then we began with the Book of Mormon, since it would be the Church's course of study the following year.

Dave was already a popular speaker, so we knew the concept would be fairly successful, but we truly had no idea it would explode into becoming one of the top-selling series in the history of LDS publishing. Those books have brought the scriptures to life for hundreds of thousands of readers.

Dave truly earned his success, though. I think only Janette and I really understood how much time and effort he was putting into each volume.

When I see the series still being advertised in the Deseret Book catalog 15 years later, I ask myself, "Is there really someone out there who hasn't bought those books yet?" I suppose a new generation is discovering them.

A Deceased Relative Gives Thanks

Around this time I had a nagging feeling that someone had been forgotten during our research on Tammy's family line. Through a series of little miracles, we discovered a woman named Rachel Marlar who had indeed been overlooked during our earlier efforts.

Several years had passed since the temple work had been done for Rachel's parents and siblings, and I received the impression she was very anxious to join her family in Paradise.

We submitted Rachel's name for temple work, and Tammy's brother Mike went to the Provo Temple with his daughter to complete the baptism and confirmation, and they could feel Rachel's presence nearby. Later in the week, Tammy completed her endowment work, and then Rachel was sealed to her parents.

The unusual part came two days later when Rachel appeared to Tammy's grandma Lucille, who wasn't even aware we were doing Rachel's temple work. Rachel stood at the end of Lucille's bed as a spirit dressed in white and shared how grateful she was that she could join her family in Paradise.

One interesting fact is that soon after Rachel visited Lucille, we found an actual photo of her taken in the 1800s. Lucille saw the photo and verified that the woman in the photo was the same person who visited her as a spirit. It was a special witness of the power of temple work. That is the reason the main family in my novel *Chasing Paradise* has the last name of Marlar, and why a woman named Lucille is a key character.

Lucille had endured many trials in her life, including being widowed in middle age. She had her favorite swear words and a quick-trigger temper, but she loved her grandkids and made the best of her situation.

After the special experience with Rachel occurred, Lucille and I spent a lot of time talking about her ancestors and how she was eager to see them. Our talks helped her remember a few more details about her heritage, and it helped us find additional names to take to the temple.

Her health began to fail, and she passed away in 2005. But it wasn't the last time I'd hear from Lucille.

This slightly ghostly image is fitting, because this is Rachel Marlar, whose temple work had been overlooked. When the ordinances were finally completed, Rachel appeared to Tammy's grandma Lucille to thank her.

CHAPTER EIGHTEEN

Spring Creek Books

By early 2004, I had been on the publishing treadmill at Cedar Fort for three years. We continued to produce great books, and I loved working with Lee and Georgia, but I needed a mental break, and I didn't see one in sight. We were releasing so many titles each month that it felt like I had more deadlines to meet than I'd had working at the Standard-Examiner.

One evening I left the office late, feeling like I was finally getting caught up. Then I returned in the morning, and Lee had put several more accepted manuscripts on my chair.

I just kind of snapped. I went home and told Tammy I'd had enough. She certainly understood. I wrote a resignation letter and put it on the owner's desk. I had no immediate plans of what to do next, but I planned on calling Access Computer Products and see if I could work for them again.

Cedar Fort's owner was obviously not happy with my letter, and we tried to negotiate how to improve my work situation. Cedar Fort made me a pretty good offer, but I just couldn't commit to going back. I went to the temple about it, and a voice told me to start my own publishing company. My first reaction was, "Oh, come on! No! That's absurd."

I truly felt I had served a three-year mission in the LDS

publishing industry, and I was now ready to try something else. As I argued with the Spirit, I was promised that if I started a new publishing company, in five years my family would be much better off than we were then.

I didn't feel that was really much of a promise, because I knew the upheaval and strife that would come from starting a rival LDS company. I finally agreed to at least look into it.

I went home and told Tammy about the guidance I'd received at the temple. She wasn't very happy about the idea. She knew better than anyone how challenging it would be, because she would have to be the company accountant.

Tammy finally agreed to pray about it. In response, she had the strongest spiritual confirmation of her life that we should move forward with it.

We formed Spring Creek Book Company the following month. Cedar Fort wasn't willing to give me the rights to my previous titles, although they would continue to carry them and pay my royalties. I also wasn't legally allowed to sign any of their authors, which was understandable.

So to begin with I was Spring Creek's only author. Thankfully the LDS book industry was at its zenith right then, and as word spread about Spring Creek, we received a flood of good manuscripts to choose from. We hired Tammy's mom Phyllis as our sales director, and her many years of retail experience paid off. She built a great rapport with the LDS store managers across the country, and we were soon off and running.

By the end of 2004, we had published 24 books written by several talented authors. We published a variety of books ranging from novels to sports books to helpful LDS non-fiction books such as *Bright Ideas for Young Women Leaders*, which is still our bestselling title.

We quickly moved into a top position in the market. We were selling so many books that we had to move to a large warehouse in Provo's East Bay to stock our inventory and keep up with the orders.

The LDS bookstores acknowledged our efforts by naming our company the Small Wholesaler of the Year at the LDS Bookseller Convention in both 2005 and 2006. We considered these awards to be a great honor, since there were dozens of small wholesalers in the LDS market at the time.

We seemed to time our book releases just right. I enjoyed publishing books such as football star quarterback Alex Smith's biography, written by Heather Simonsen. We debuted his book at a booksigning at the University of Utah Bookstore the week after he was selected No. 1 in the 2005 NFL Draft. We had a line of Ute fans snaking through the aisles and out the store door. We sold more than 500 copies in three hours. It was crazy, fun times.

I also contacted a few LDS celebrities to write their autobiographies, and this led to multiple bestsellers. American Idol finalist Carmen Rasmusen wrote a wonderful book aimed at young women entitled *Staying in Tune* that sold thousands of copies.

Miss America contestant Jill Stevens' book *It's All Good* also topped the bestseller lists with her story of serving in the U.S. military before becoming Miss Utah. Both books contained inspiring messages that readers loved.

Working with Suzanne Freeman

Soon after I established the book company, I was contacted by my friend Shirley Bahlmann, who is also an author. A woman named Suzanne Freeman had approached her at a booksigning and told her about having a near-death experience. She was feeling prompted to somehow share her experience more publicly, even though she was a shy person and was very reluctant to do so.

Above: The biography of college football star Alex Smith, written by Heather Simonsen, was a big seller for us. Their booksigning at the U of U bookstore was a huge success.

Right: My daughter Emma enjoyed meeting many of our authors, particularly American Idol finalist Carmen Rasmusen, shown here at a Costco event.

Shirley met with her, took some notes, and came away impressed by Suzanne's account. She then called me to see if I'd be interested in publishing Suzanne's story. Less than a week later I drove to Ephraim, Utah and met Suzanne at Shirley's home. She gave me a brief synopsis of her near-death experience, then I asked her if she'd read other near-death accounts, wondering if she had "borrowed" some ideas from those stories.

She shook her head, explaining that she was a housewife with several children that occupied all of her time. She was familiar with the basic truths of her LDS faith, but she said she wasn't a gospel scholar. She even mentioned she'd had dyslexia as a child and that reading still didn't come easily to her. I felt confident Suzanne was telling me the truth—that a humble housewife from a small Utah town had actually died, met the Savior, and returned.

However, before I'd even consider publishing her story, I wanted to make sure her account stayed consistent within itself. I began asking her many questions to see if she would slip up or change her story, but throughout the "interrogation" she looked me in the eyes and was straightforward with her answers. After thirty minutes, I felt satisfied and said, "I believe you. I feel we should publish your experience."

Suzanne seemed uncertain whether she had heard me correctly. "Really?" she asked. "You believe me?"

She then explained she'd been ridiculed within her family and in her community for even mentioning her experience, and she'd expected the same outcome from our meeting. I assured her that I believed her. Shirley joined us in the front room, and she agreed to help write the book. Within a few months *Led by the Hand of Christ* was published, which told of Suzanne's various experiences while in the Spirit World.

Suzanne had also been shown a series of troubling future world events while on the other side. At first I pushed Suzanne to include these events in her book, but even talking about them caused her great distress, so I backed off. I sensed she had been shown those events for a reason, and possibly the time would come later for her to share them.

Led by the Hand of Christ sold well throughout 2005, and Suzanne spoke to several groups about her experience. As the months passed, she felt more comfortable with describing the troubling future events she'd been shown by the Savior. She collaborated again with Shirley on another book that shared what she had seen, and *Through the Window of Life* was released in 2006. It also became a bestseller.

I greatly appreciate Suzanne and her willingness to share her experiences. She helped pave the way for my own futuristic novels and similar books we have published.

Writing the Standing in Holy Places Series

After working with Suzanne, I knew I needed to write my *Standing in Holy Places* series. I had been prompted to start this series ever since forming the book company. The series would tell in fictional form the future events concerning my children that I had been shown by Grandpa Keith when I left my body at La Jolla Cove.

As I have explained, my veil never closed up again after that second near-death experience, and over the years I had compiled in my mind dozens of future scenes regarding my family. I felt prompted that the first novel should be called *The Great Gathering* and should be set more than a decade in the future.

Frankly, I didn't want to do it. It didn't feel like the right time to release a novel about the decline and downfall of the United States.

In 2006, writing about deplorable future conditions in America seemed ludicrous to even consider. People were building bigger houses, buying new cars, and loading up their 0% interest credit cards. Everyone was prospering!

At that time, the Middle East was relatively calm after the execution of Saddam Hussein. The thought of terrorist groups gaining power seemed impossible. Russia and China were keeping low profiles, and the United States was seemingly in control of the world.

I've saved an article from that year that quoted President George W. Bush. He had visited Wall Street and hailed the "strong state of the economy." He went on to say, "America's businesses and entrepreneurs are creating new jobs every day. Workers are making more money; their paychecks are going further. Consumers are confident, investors are optimistic."

I continued to drag my feet on the novel, but my signal to devote my full attention to it came one morning when I traveled to Sanpete County during the annual Manti Pageant. Our company had a booth there where we sold books to visitors. That morning I passed the McDonalds restaurant on the south end of Ephraim and soon could see the Manti Temple in the distance. There were miles of empty fields to the west.

Then it was like I was suddenly in a different time. I saw thousands of tents in those fields. They were clearly organized into blocks with wide pathways between them. I saw hundreds of people of all ages outside the tents. Some were performing chores, while others were walking toward the temple. The people seemed calm and happy.

Then I nearly swerved off the road, which brought me back to the present day. The fields were empty again, but I took it as a message that I needed to get working on *The Great Gathering*. I knew the vision I had received needed to be included in the novel. In fact, the book's cover image of a young girl in a wheat field is similar to what I was shown that day.

As I worked on the novel, I would have glimpses of the Oval

Office, but I would only see the back of the U.S. president's chair. I never saw his face, but I heard his speaking cadence and the phrases he used. It certainly wasn't President George W. Bush. I knew I was writing about a future U.S. president.

Along those lines, it was strange to write about President Gordon B. Hinckley's funeral in the opening segment. Readers rush right past that part now, but when I wrote that, he was still a vibrant, healthy man. He didn't pass away until long after the novel had been released.

I suppose I know how the writers of the movie *Back to the Future II* must have felt as they tried to accurately portray what life would be like in 2015. When they sent Marty McFly and Doc Brown into the future, they were incorrect on a few things—flying cars, the movie *Jaws 19*, and so on—but at least they had fun with it.

That's what I attempted to do with the sport called Conquest in the book. I did see the traditional major sports leagues shutting down, but violent sports continued to thrive. We see the sports world heading in that direction as the top Mixed Martial Arts events now often overshadow traditional sports.

The most challenging part for me was writing about the upcoming foreign invasion of America. I had been shown several different snippets of destruction and terror in bigger U.S. cities, and then the invaders began moving inland. I did specifically see the scene where the tanks go into Spanish Fork Canyon, only to have their path blocked. It helped me realize the Saints in Sanpete County would be protected.

I didn't feel I could write extensively about the invasion, though, because I hadn't been shown many specific details. The military scenes I saw were mainly a montage of vehicles rolling through large cities and then rapidly spreading across the country.

Dad helped edit the novel, and he pointed out that it seemed like I really rushed through that part. We talked about expanding it, but that night the Spirit told me, "That's enough for now. A time will come when you can write about it with greater clarity."

I had no idea what that answer meant, but it has been fulfilled in my new *Times of Turmoil* series. The first three volumes all take place within the same time frame as *The Great Gathering*. I've been able to slow down the pace and better explain how the United Nations and the invading armies will work together to attack America.

The Great Gathering actually sold really well right from the start, and when the Great Recession hit in 2008, many readers wondered if the things I described in my book were already starting to happen.

Deep down I knew we were still several years away, though, because one of the key parts of the book involves the government encouraging human microchip implants. The technology exists now and is being encouraged by private businesses.

The following year I wrote a second volume in the series entitled *The Celestial City*, and I envisioned a completed series of five volumes. But real life soon invaded my writing schedule, and I wasn't sure I would ever write another novel.

I collaborated with my talented cousin Rhett Murray on the illustrated book "Through the Eyes of John." The book describes the Savior's final days from the perspective of his beloved apostle. Rhett's paintings graced the covers of several of our books, including Suzanne Freeman's "Led by the Hand of Christ."

Right: Tammy's mom Phyllis Douglas was a key part to Spring Creek's success. As our company salesperson, she built strong relationships with the managers of LDS bookstores across the country.

CHAPTER NINETEEN

※

Company Collapse

By early 2008, there were dark clouds on the bookselling horizon. There was talk of the economy slowing down, but at our annual LDS Booksellers convention I heard my fellow publishers and store owners reassure each other that everything was going to be okay.

A popular statement I often heard was, "During the Great Depression, book sales actually increased, because people still wanted to be entertained."

Well, history didn't repeat itself in this case. Customers had many other ways to entertain themselves in 2008 than they did in the 1930s. By September our book sales came to a standstill. It became evident the nation really had entered a recession.

Customers quit buying books, and the bookstore owners panicked. They started sending hundreds of books back to us and demanding credit for them. It was a nightmare. Tammy and I saw the writing on the wall. As the economic problems continued throughout the nation, it was clear I needed to find a full-time job to support our family.

We essentially put Spring Creek into hibernation. I turned over our remaining inventory to Brigham Distributing, and they shipped out our books whenever someone ordered them, which wasn't very often. I realized it had been four and a half years since the Spirit had told me my family would be better off in five years. I was admittedly bitter, because the chance of that prompting coming true looked very unlikely.

We scraped by financially, and Tammy took a part-time job as the computer lab teacher at Art City Elementary School. Then I heard Spanish Fork's cemetery sexton was going to retire. I applied for the job in November, but more than 150 people had applied, and I eventually gave up on even getting an interview for the job. Then around Christmas I was notified I'd been selected as one of the final candidates.

In January 2009 I went through a series of interviews with the department heads of Spanish Fork City. After a tense few days, I received the call I'd been selected for the position.

The starting salary was a pleasant surprise. I would be paid better than I ever had, with great insurance. I started the job on January 26th in the middle of a blizzard, and I was trained by the previous sexton for four days. Then I was on my own, but things went well and I soon settled into the job. Suddenly I was working about 50 hours a week at the cemetery, clearing snow and digging graves.

When I started the Spanish Fork Cemetery job, the promise of the Spirit had been fulfilled almost five years to the day. With our two new jobs, we were indeed better off financially than we were in February 2004.

We were grateful for the new jobs, although in some ways the whole scenario felt like a cruel trick. In reality, both Tammy and I were still in shock at how quickly the book company had fallen apart. We had felt so guided and inspired to start the company, and then less than five years later Spring Creek was seemingly done.

The company's collapse had really taken a toll on Tammy. She was our Chief Financial Officer and took the brunt of the financial stress. She didn't smile for a long time, and she showed the symptoms of having suffered a mental breakdown. It was definitely the most challenging phase of our marriage, and we both needed a break from the publishing industry. We wanted to put it in the rearview mirror and never look back.

However, I gave her a special priesthood blessing at the time that strengthened both of us. During the blessing I was shown Tammy in the premortal world. I saw her in a beautiful white dress vigorously defending the Plan of Salvation to a large group of spirits during the War in Heaven. Then the scene changed and I saw her teaching a class of spirits in a large auditorium. I knew she was one of Heavenly Father's most valiant children. We had been put through a very tough test, but I assured her we would make it through and be stronger for it.

In the vision, Tammy had long brown hair. Her hair turned darker after she gave birth to Garth, and she now looks more like her premortal self than at any other point in her life.

Nearly Giving Up Writing

When the company collapsed, I had written the first two volumes of my *Standing in Holy Places* series, and in my frustration I was ready to call it quits on that project too. However, the Spanish Fork cemetery secretary, Marty Warren, started reading my books and became a great support to me.

Whenever I would take the cemetery paperwork to Marty at the city offices, she would say, "When is that next book coming out?" or "I need more books. I gave them to my friends to read."

She really was a powerful motivator. So I would go home at night and make some progress on the books, eventually finishing the series over the next two years.

CHAPTER TWENTY

Spanish Fork Cemetery

In some ways it was surreal that I was suddenly the Spanish Fork cemetery sexton. When you grow up in Springville, your main rival is Spanish Fork. So it was an adjustment to work there, but I had some great co-workers, and I started to bounce back and enjoy life again.

My Employees See a Boy Spirit

Most days at the cemetery were fairly mundane, but every once in a while we had some ghostly experiences. I want to share a situation where I didn't see anything, but my two co-workers did! I'll call them Derik and Sam to protect their privacy. They've told the story many times, but it has been a few years and maybe they're tired of talking about it.

We were filling a grave in a part of the cemetery where many original settlers were buried. Once the vault was in the ground, I drove the backhoe to our dirt pile a few hundred yards away.

When I returned with a scoop of dirt, I saw Derik and Sam both backing away from the grave. Sam was pointing at something, and Derik actually hid behind Sam.

At that point the backhoe was close enough that they turned to look at me. Something had clearly spooked them. I dumped the dirt in the grave, then turned off the machine and hopped out. Derik and Sam started shoveling the dirt as if nothing had happened, but then Sam asked me, "Did you see him too?"

"What do you mean?" I asked. They looked at each other in surprise. Sam stammered for a moment before walking to a spot about ten feet from the grave. "There was a boy standing right here," Sam said. "He was watching us."

Derik said, "Yeah, he was probably eight years old and about four feet tall. He had on some clothes like from the Great Depression. But he vanished when you got closer with the backhoe."

As he said that, I felt a little freaked out as well. "Could you see through him?" I asked.

They both shook their heads. "I thought he was a real kid at first," Derik said. "He had dark hair, but his skin looked kind of gray. He stood there for at least thirty seconds."

"He actually looked kind of mad," Sam added. "I was glad he disappeared when you drove back over here!"

We discussed that boy many times during the rest of the summer. The interesting thing to me is that both Derik and Sam saw him. I checked the cemetery records, and there were three young boys buried in that area who died in the 1930s. So maybe one of them just wanted to stop by and see how things were going!

My Friend Don's Remarkable Story

I became acquainted with a man I'll call Don. He was in his 70s, and his wife had passed away two years earlier. He would visit her grave often, and we would often chat. Don knew my dad from their days at Geneva Steel, and he'd sometimes help me out if I was filling a grave.

Don is one of the happiest people I know, but not long ago

he was a bitter, broken man. As we got to be close friends, he told me his story.

The first year after his wife died, Don was absolutely heartbroken. His wife, who I'll call Karen, had died of cancer, and she had suffered greatly during the last months of her life. She and Don had been sealed in the temple many years earlier, but they'd been inactive in the Church for decades.

After Karen's death, Don's grief basically incapacitated him. He told me the only reason he got out of bed each day after Karen passed away was to drive to the cemetery.

Then one day while at Karen's grave, Don heard her voice! She told him she was doing fine and that he needed to get back to living a normal life again. She said his grief was actually affecting her ability to work in the Spirit World, and she had received permission to speak to him.

Here's the part I find very interesting. About a week after telling me the full story, he waved me down and said, "How come you didn't tell me you are an author?"

I shrugged and said, "You never asked."

Don smiled. "Well, Karen had told me you wrote a book that would really help me understand what she is doing in the Spirit World."

"Maybe she's talking about my novel *Chasing Paradise*," I said.

He clapped his hands together. "That's it! Can you get me a copy?"

I brought him the book the next day, and he returned it a few days later. "Thank you," Don said. "I read it twice. Your book makes everything so much clearer. Karen told me she's working as a secretary there, and it kind of blew my mind. We've been inactive most of our lives, so I honestly wondered if Karen was somewhere else, if you know what I mean."

Karen had explained to him that she helped schedule classes

for people who had accepted the gospel in Spirit Prison. She told Don that she arranges the seating in massive classrooms, where wonderful gospel teachers such as Parley P. Pratt and others give powerful sermons. Karen said hundreds of thousands of people in her portion of the Spirit World alone have accepted the gospel, but they feel stuck in their progression until their temple work is done.

Don and Karen's story is fascinating, and she has continued to communicate with him. One of their daughters died unexpectedly, and Karen assured Don that their daughter was now working with her in a similar capacity.

That formerly inactive man is now an "unofficial" temple worker. He refused to accept an assigned position because they wouldn't give him enough scheduled hours each week. Instead, he goes to the temple four times a week on his own and stays throughout the day. What a remarkable man!

Cemetery Visions

Some of my most powerful visions have occurred when I was operating a weedeater to trim around headstones. I suppose it was because my mind was basically unoccupied and could be filled with heavenly knowledge. There were many times I often snapped out of a vision to find myself still holding the weedeater a few feet from where I last remembered standing. Too bad no one ever caught me on video. I'm sure it would be entertaining to watch!

Many of these visions were very sacred and aren't appropriate to include in this book. They often included short memories of my premortal life, and also glimpses of my role within my extended family as the Second Coming approaches. Many of these visions are incorporated in the final two volumes of my *Standing in Holy Places* series, though.

I'm surprised I was able to smile in this photo. A storm dumped 20 inches of snow on the Spanish Fork Cemetery in December 2009. The snow broke large branches off hundreds of trees. Other city employees helped me haul away loads of limbs for several weeks to get the cemetery back in order.

Church Service

My Church service through the years has been varied and interesting, including serving as Scoutmaster in four different wards. (I'm hoping I've experienced my last Klondike Derby.)

I enjoyed serving in callings such as Elders Quorum President, Bishopric First Counselor, Stake Young Men First Counselor, and I'm currently the Ward Executive Secretary for a second time.

In other words, I'm just like my Daybell ancestors—a good serviceable member of the stake. My torn veil actually came in handy many times while I was in the bishopric in regard to receiving inspiration.

For example, I was stopped at an intersection and waved to an older neighbor lady who was crossing the street. The Spirit said, "There's the next Primary president."

She hadn't been on our list, but when I suggested her name to the bishop at our next meeting, he nodded thoughtfully, and the Spirit confirmed the calling for us when we prayed about it.

That happened time and again. An inactive brother was repairing my car when the Spirit said, "He sure would be a great Assistant Cubmaster."

The Spirit was correct. That man had a blast in the calling and brought delicious treats to every Pack Meeting.

I love the gospel of Jesus Christ, and the LDS Church and my family are my top priorities. But like most of you who sometimes have two callings at once, I actually wouldn't mind a week off once in a while. Most of the time I was called to the next position before I was released from the previous one. The one time I thought I'd get a rest was when I was released from the bishopric.

The next Sunday I wore a white short-sleeve shirt, khaki pants, and a really colorful tie to church. A lot of people smiled and commented how strange it was to see me not wearing a suit. It didn't last long, though. Before the day was over, I was called into the Stake Young Men Presidency, and I was wearing my suit again the next week. The break was fun while it lasted!

CHAPTER TWENTY-ONE

※

Lucille Gets Feisty

While working at the Spanish Fork Cemetery I felt an urgency to begin working on the Marlar family line again, and it was amazing how the obstacles we had faced previously in finding Tammy's ancestors were now cleared away.

However, Tammy struggled to get motivated about it. She'd found a new hobby—Frontierville, a spinoff of the online computer game Farmville. She was spending a few hours each day building fictional online towns. I was hoping she would soon get bored with it.

I went to the temple and received a strong impression to tell Tammy she needed to stop playing Frontierville "cold turkey." I did as I had been prompted, and we had a good discussion about it. Tammy knew the game had become an addiction, but she didn't fully stop. She didn't resume working on family history, either.

Two months later, on September 23, 2011, I was working on the Marlar line and found the records of several families while Tammy and the kids were visiting her parents. I could feel the Spirit strongly.

Then I felt a presence standing behind my right shoulder, and into my mind came Grandma Lucille's voice. It was a younger voice than when I had known her, but it was definitely her.

"You can't do this alone," Lucille said. "It's time for those who have stewardship to get off their butts."

Lucille explained to me that she was working in the Spirit World as a missionary. She added that as the only deceased member in her family who had been a member of the LDS Church on earth, she had the responsibility to prompt her descendants to do the temple work.

I felt Lucille motion toward the Osborne County, Kansas history book on the desk. She said, "There are thousands of spirits waiting to move to Paradise, but they're stuck in the Spirit Prison until their temple work is done. Most of the people in that book have accepted the gospel and are waiting for our family to do their work. That book is the key. It was compiled by inspiration many years ago. All of the families in there are interconnected through direct bloodlines and marriage."

I was then shown in my mind a ball similar to the one that drops in Times Square on New Year's Eve. The ball was made up of hundreds of interconnected pieces of glass. I understood that each family is comparable to a piece of glass. Each one is needed to make the ball complete.

Lucille then continued, "We've explained to these ancestors that their work will eventually be done, but it's frustrating to them that the information is right here being ignored. They feel spiritually starved. They know there's a big feast waiting for them, but they can't cross the gulf into Paradise yet."

Then her voice got louder and angrier. (This was the Lucille I remembered!) She said, "My descendants are letting Satan lull them to sleep with technology. Two months ago in the temple I told you to have Tammy quit her d*** computer game cold turkey so she would be receptive to a message from me, but she didn't. She has more important work to do than play games. We need her desperately."

She then gave me several instructions to tell Tammy, including that she needed to get her mother Phyllis involved in doing the work.

I quickly opened up a Word document on the computer and typed in everything she was telling me. I felt Lucille's presence linger until I finished. Then she said, "Go tell them right now. It's not your job to do our family's work. You've got books to write."

That was a wake-up call for me as well. I'd finished the *Standing in Holy Places* series that summer, and I didn't have anything new in mind. But after Lucille's admonition, I started an outline for my *Times of Turmoil* series later that week.

Anyway, I printed off Lucille's message and called Tammy to come home. I had her read through the message, and she took it pretty well. Then we went back to visit Phyllis. I'd never told my in-laws too much about my spiritual gifts, so it was going to be a curious conversation.

They were watching TV in the living room, and I asked them to turn it off. Then I held up the paper and said, "Phyllis, your mom Lucille just visited me. She had a few things to say."

Phyllis read it, and she and Tammy both started crying, but in a good way. They agreed that Lucille's use of the "d" word was the true sign they needed!

Then Phyllis sat up straight and said, "You know what? Today is her birthday. Maybe this was her gift to herself." We all got chills as that sunk in.

Lucille's message worked. Tammy quit playing Frontierville, and she and Phyllis have done a monumental work over the past few years. Thousands of names have been submitted to the temple, and I know those people are moving into Paradise.

I have had a few other encounters with Lucille since then, and she is in a much better mood now. One time was in the Provo Temple when several of her grandchildren were being baptized and confirmed for their ancestors. I saw her in a spiritual portal that connected to the confirmation room we were in. She was assisting spirits in and out of the room as their work was being done. She had a big smile on her face!

Vision of Children Fulfilled

Over the years I often thought about the vision I had seen in Ogden of all five children together on a happy occasion dressed in church clothes. It was so implanted on my mind that it had been a little eerie to see the kids become the people I'd envisioned before they were even born.

However, I'd never seen all five kids together at once like I had in the vision. When Garth departed on his mission to Oklahoma in 2011, Mark was still a small boy. Then Emma left on her mission to Tennessee before Garth returned. With the lowering of mission ages, Seth was getting ready to leave on his mission in June, before Emma got home. It looked like we'd have a stretch of nearly six years without having all five children home at the same time. I began to wonder if the dream was merely symbolic.

Then we received word that Emma had contracted a serious illness on her mission and needed to return home a few months early. We picked her up at the airport in December 2013, and she was pale and weak. It took her several months to recover.

Meanwhile, Seth had received his mission call to Virginia. The night that Seth was set apart as a missionary, the five kids all put on mission badges and posed together. As I watched them from ten feet away, I got emotional, realizing this was the moment I had seen in my vision. I was so grateful Mark had not been forgotten!

Our five children on the night Seth (in the middle) was set apart as a missionary. As I watched them, my vision from more than two decades earlier was fulfilled. Mark had not been forgotten!

The photo on the left is Grandma Lucille a year before she passed away. The photo on the right was taken during her younger years. When I visit with her now, her spirit appears like her younger self. She is working hard in the Spirit World and isn't letting us slack off on this side of the veil.

CHAPTER TWENTY-TWO

❧

Recent Spiritual Books

There was one aspect of the Spring Creek's collapse that really bothered me. Soon after we published Suzanne Freeman's book *Through the Window of Life* in 2006, I had a vision of a tall, dark-haired woman who would publish her near-death experience with our company.

It was a full waking vision of her speaking to a large group in an elegant building with balcony seating, and I was sitting near her as she spoke. She had a distinctive voice that I would recognize anywhere.

Yet now I was essentially out of the publishing business. I expected to be Spanish Fork's cemetery sexton until I retired, but something strange happened. We still had about twenty books in print, and as the economy improved, these older titles were suddenly selling better than they had when we first released them.

I started speaking to book clubs around the valley, and my earlier novels found a new audience. The sales revenue still wasn't enough for me to leave my full-time job, but it gave me hope that maybe the company could bounce back. I still had that dark-haired woman in the back of my mind I had seen in vision several years earlier.

I have actually refused to publish several near-death books over the years. I followed the Spirit on those decisions. Sometimes the experience itself measured up as authentic, but if an author seemed too focused on making money or gaining fame, I would put the brakes on the project.

In other cases the authors would seem like good people, but their manuscripts would leave me with serious concerns about the source of the material. I would sincerely ponder and pray if these experiences were meant to be published to the world. Many times the answer from the Spirit would be a strong warning of "Steer clear."

I haven't seen any of these books get published elsewhere, so I'm grateful for the guidance I received to not publish them.

A Greater Tomorrow

There have been a few great experiences, though. In January 2014, I was checking a preparedness website when I saw a post by a woman named Julie Rowe who said she felt she should share her near-death experience. She asked if anyone knew someone who might be able to help publish her experience. I thought, "I do."

I sent her a basic email explaining that I was the president of Spring Creek Books and I would be interested in hearing her story. We exchanged a couple of emails, and then I called her to make the conversation easier. I still didn't know what she looked like, but I recognized the distinctive voice. She had a Facebook page at the time, and I looked up her photo after we talked. It was the tall, dark-haired woman I had seen!

Julie began working on her manuscript, and it came together quite rapidly, even though she lived in Arizona and I was in Utah. Her book *A Greater Tomorrow* was released in mid-May. I never even met Julie in person until mid-July when our families got together at BYU's Bean Museum.

Later that same week Julie spoke in the Logan Tabernacle to several hundred people. As I sat near her on the stand while she addressed the crowd in that historic building, the vision was fulfilled.

Tammy and I faced a curious dilemma in creating Julie's book cover, because Julie had actually seen the book in her vision of the future. She tried to describe the cover to me, and she mentioned a field of red flowers. I'm usually the one who finds the cover images for Spring Creek's books, and in this case I searched through hundreds of images of red flowers on a couple of photo websites.

I finally found one that was similar to her description, but I knew it wasn't right. I gave up and went to bed, only to awake with a start in the middle of the night. A voice said, "The image is there now."

I went out to the computer, opened the photo site, and typed in "field of red flowers." The image was right there on the first page. Tammy assembled the cover the next day and sent it to Julie, who quickly responded, "That's it! That's amazing!"

Julie's second book, *The Time is Now*, was written in a similar manner, including another heavenly intervention in finding the right cover image. That book focuses on the words of the prophets concerning the latter days, with additional insights from Julie on future events. She also gives advice on how to spiritually and temporally prepare for troubles that are coming.

Julie is a humble, kind person who simply seeks to do the Lord's will. The books have blessed many lives in helping people recognize and understand the Lord's love for each of us.

She has received severe opposition at times, but I see that as a testament that she's on the right course and is spreading a message of truth. I appreciate her courage and faithfulness.

Hector Sosa

A couple of months after Julie's second book was released, I was visiting with my family at home in Springville when the Spirit said, "Go knock on Hector Sosa's door right now. He needs to write a book."

I really hate receiving those kinds of messages. Hector had posted some messages on a website about visions he'd had about the future, but I hadn't considered approaching him about writing a book. After all, I knew how writing a book can change a person's life completely, in both good and bad ways.

I had never met Hector or even sent him an email message, but after hearing that voice I went to the computer and found his address. I was happy to see he also lived in Springville. At least the Spirit knew it would be a short trip. I was expecting him to live in Provo or even farther.

I grabbed my jacket and told Tammy, "Uh, I need to go tell someone they need to write a book." She is fortunately accustomed to this kind of thing.

"Okay," she said. "I'll see you when you get back."

It was dark by the time I got to Hector's home. I rang the doorbell, and Hector opened the door a bit tentatively. I said, "Hi, I'm Chad Daybell. I publish Julie Rowe's books. You've heard of her, right?"

Hector nodded. "Yeah, I've read her books."

"Can I come in for a minute?" I asked. Hector graciously allowed me in, and I explained I had read some of his dreams on a website. He shared more details about them, and we really felt like old friends right from the start. I met his wife, who is also named Tammy, and I thought that was a good sign. After a half hour, I finally broached the subject of writing a book. Hector looked shocked. "Me?" he asked. "Wow, I don't know."

I figured that answer was better than "No." So I explained

how I would help assemble it. He soon agreed to do it, and I made sure his wife Tammy was on board as well. They are a great couple, and she has been a huge support every step of the way.

Over the next couple of weeks, Hector wrote a very good first draft. Then we started meeting every Thursday evening, and he would give me more material for the manuscript. During these meetings I would ask additional questions that helped him remember certain dreams and visions. These visits brought forth some of the most powerful parts of his book *A Change is Coming*.

Interesting Dreams about Scott Mitchell

As I explained earlier, NFL star quarterback Scott Mitchell and I were friends growing up—not buddies who hung out together, but definitely friends. He and I were often on the same basketball and baseball teams, and his dad Bill was usually our coach.

I had closely followed Scott's football career. He went on to excel at the University of Utah, setting several NCAA passing records. The Miami Dolphins then drafted him in 1990, and he spent three years as Dan Marino's backup.

When Dan suffered a season-ending injury early in the 1993 season, Scott came in and led the team to several victories. He became a free agent and signed with the Detroit Lions, where he teamed up with Hall of Fame running back Barry Sanders for several seasons.

One of my favorite Thanksgiving Day memories was in 1995 when Scott led the Lions to a comeback victory over the Minnesota Vikings. He threw for more than 400 yards and four touchdowns that day, and everyone in Springville was smiling.

He ended his career with the Baltimore Ravens and the Cincinnati Bengals before moving to Orlando, Florida and doing well in the world of real estate. It seemed he had left

Springville behind for good.

After I formed Spring Creek Books in 2004, though, I began having dreams that involved publishing a book with Scott. I would have them every month or so out of the blue. There was one very strange part to the dreams—Scott was really skinny, almost like when we were in high school.

That really stood out to me, because after his NFL career, "skinny" is not a word you would have used to describe Scott. He had gained a lot of weight.

In 2008 he surprised everyone when he moved from Florida and accepted the job as football coach at Springville High. He coached for four years and led the program back to prominence. Meanwhile, his weight kept increasing.

After Scott moved back to Springville, we talked a few times about publishing his life story. The timing didn't feel right, though. Plus, my vision of a skinny Scott was just not possible. It would take an absolute miracle for him to match what I had seen.

Then Scott's dad Bill passed away from obesity-related issues, and Scott had several meaningful experiences that indicated he needed to change his life. Scott had ballooned to 366 pounds, and he could see himself following his father's path.

He decided to audition for the TV show *The Biggest Loser* and was accepted as a cast member. He soon became a focal point of the season as he confronted family and personal challenges.

Scott was on his way to losing 124 pounds, and he miraculously looked like the guy I had seen in my dreams many years earlier.

When there were two episodes of the show left to air, I felt a strong prompting to contact Scott. I sent him a Facebook message asking, "Is it time we finally do your book?"

He quickly responded that he'd been having the same impression. He happened to be in Utah for a short break before

The Biggest Loser finale, so I went to his home and showed him the variety of books Spring Creek had produced over the years. We talked for two hours, and it was great to reconnect.

Other publishers were interested in his story, of course, and Scott listened to their offers. I waited nervously for a few days for him to make his decision, but he finally called me and said, "Let's go for it!"

We took an unusual route in producing Scott's book. We had a court reporter come to Scott's home. She typed away while Scott told us his story. He really opened up and shared a lot of things that I'd never known before. I would occasionally ask him questions when we needed clarification, but for the most part he just talked through the key moments of his life, such as how an answered prayer led him to attend the U of U instead of BYU.

Seven hours later, we essentially had the book's contents. We came up with the fitting title *Alive Again*. Scott spent a couple of weeks adding stories and refining the text while I double-checked game scores and other details. His wife Wendy was a great help in shaping the manuscript, and she helped select the photos that are inside the book.

I'm so happy with how the book turned out. He included several spiritual experiences you wouldn't have expected from a tough football player. It's the true "hero's journey." Scott let his obesity take him into the depths of despair, but he fought back and is truly alive again. It is so rewarding to hear how his journey has touched so many lives.

Time to Move On

I was really enjoying working with these authors, but I again faced the same problem I encountered fifteen years earlier. I was working at the cemetery during the day and editing these books at night. It had finally became too time-consuming.

I had a good time with Scott Mitchell at the 2015 U of U Spring Game. Scott threw three touchdown passes during the alumni game, then greeted hundreds of fans afterward at a booksigning.

I had basically served two five-year terms as a cemetery sexton. I worked for Springville City from 1995 to 2000 before moving on to other jobs. Then I was Spanish Fork's sexton from 2009 to 2013, before returning to Springville for a year.

I finally resigned as Springville's sexton in 2014 and worked with my brother-in-law Jason Gwilliam for several months. He owns a window installation company, and working with him three or four days a week gave me more flexibility to work on the books.

I don't think I'll ever return to the cemetery. It's a challenging profession, both physically and emotionally. A drawback to the job is that my daily life was pretty much in the hands of the local mortuaries. If I planned to attend a special event, it was almost guaranteed someone would pass away and the funeral would be scheduled at the same time. I could sometimes get a co-worker to cover for me, but often it felt like the Grim Reaper was checking our family's calendar and doing his best to disrupt our plans.

I did like many aspects of the job. I enjoyed the friendships with my co-workers and helping visitors locate their relatives' graves, but my sensitivity to the other side of the veil worked against me. As the years passed, the cumulative spiritual experiences began to weigh me down. I guess the phrase "emotional baggage" is a fair description of what I was dealing with.

Each day at the cemetery would add another pebble to my invisible emotional backpack. The backpack just got too heavy after about five years, and leaving the sexton job was the only way I could shake off the baggage.

Sad funerals would obviously add a few extra pebbles, but I also sensed other situations, such as when a mother would come the night before and cry on her son's grave. That energy still radiated the next morning. It wasn't necessarily a dark energy, but the grief the mother felt would still weigh me down.

Traveling Along the Wasatch Front

My new window installation job with Jason actually helped hone my visionary skills. Jason would drive the window van, giving me time to sit in the passenger seat and look at the scenery.

As we drove to different locations along the Wasatch Front from Ogden to Santaquin, I received visions of what the future would soon hold for each area. There are some tough times coming.

We did a window job in Copperton on the western side of the Salt Lake Valley, and the scenes I was shown there are now a key part of my novel *Days of Fury*.

I didn't know how long I would work with Jason, but based on what I was being shown in these visions, I sensed a major change was coming for my family.

Chapter Twenty-Three

An Unexpected Move to Idaho

My mother loves to organize family get-togethers, and in August 2014 she rented a large cabin in Island Park, Idaho for the whole extended family.

On the way to the cabin, we stopped at a gas station in the town of St. Anthony, north of Rexburg. As I filled the van with gas, I looked south back over the valley. A voice simply said, "You'll live here soon."

I was genuinely surprised to receive that message. We were firmly entrenched in Springville. I was still the cemetery sexton at that time, and Tammy had just taken a secretarial position at Springville High. I knew she wouldn't respond very well to this new information, so I kept it to myself. Besides, what did "soon" mean? There was no need for Tammy to worry about it if we weren't supposed to move for a couple of years.

We spent a few fun days at Island Park riding in the boat, playing on a wave runner, and just enjoying a much-needed break from everyday life. The scenery was beautiful, and everything was so calm and laid-back. The thought of living in Idaho started to really appeal to me.

After our vacation, I went to the Provo Temple to get a confirmation about the prompting. The Spirit assured me it was true, but I was still left in the dark concerning the timing.

I was working with Hector and Scott on their books, and I knew I'd still have to be in Springville to complete those projects. However, I'd also had promptings I would be in Idaho when I finished my latest novel *Days of Fury*. So there were a lot of conflicting scenarios being presented to me. I didn't see how it would all fit together.

In early February 2015 I received another "fork in the road" vision. As I looked down the right fork, I saw in the distance a glorious city with a temple on a hill. A voice said, "Moving to Rexburg will be a tremendous blessing to your children and your grandchildren."

I glanced down the left fork and sensed it represented us not moving from Springville. That path was filled with many lost opportunities, both spiritually and financially. After this vision, I reread my children's patriarchal blessings, and each one verified what I had seen. I was still waiting for the right time to even mention it to my family, though.

A couple of weeks later, as we were eating dinner the following words slipped out of my mouth, "When we move to Rexburg . . ."

I didn't finish the sentence because I saw the look on Tammy's face. She loudly said, "What?"

Things got a little tense after that, but I explained the feelings I'd been having and how I wasn't sure how all of the projects would fit together. I said, "Maybe it won't happen for a year or two. Forget I said anything."

Tammy wasn't thrilled, and I completely understood her feelings. Moving to Idaho would be a major undertaking that would uproot us from our families. I didn't bring it up again.

Then after a few weeks Tammy felt impressed by the Spirit

that we should at least look into moving. We had learned from past experience that if we were supposed to move, things would fall into place almost magically. If we weren't supposed to move yet, nothing would work out.

Tammy started looking at real estate websites. One house north of Rexburg jumped out at us, and there was also a second home nearby that might work, so we decided to drive up to Rexburg in late March.

I called up the real estate agent for the first home, and she agreed to meet us there the following Saturday. I mentioned the second home, and she arranged for us to look at it as well.

We went to the first house, and it wasn't what had been advertised. We were very disappointed, but we decided to look at the second house. It turned out to be similar to our home in Springville, except it also had four acres of pasture and a pond.

The home needed new carpet and fresh paint, but as I walked through the pasture and discussed the house with my son Garth, we both really felt this was the place for us. Garth said, "I feel I could really thrive here."

Tammy and the other children agreed, and from that point on, everything came together quickly. We closed on the house in early June.

We had sent Scott's book to press in April and Hector's book in late May. Once we moved to Idaho, I began working on my novel *Days of Fury*. I went to the David O. McKay Library on the BYU-Idaho campus each morning and worked on it for a few hours at a time.

The final chapters seemed to be dictated to me by the Spirit, and I typed as fast as I could. It was a unique experience to be writing about the future of the BYU-Idaho Center and be able to see it out the library window as I did so.

There were many indications that this is where the Lord wanted us. The move has opened up many opportunities for me in the publishing world. We had been warned it might be hard for the other family members to immediately find employment, but we have all been able to find good jobs.

Leaving our ward in Springville was an emotional struggle. Tammy and I served in nearly every possible calling during our 18 years there. Our new ward members have treated us kindly, though, and the kids have been well accepted.

My vision of the two paths is already being fulfilled. Tammy has turned into a farmer, raising all kinds of plants and animals. It is wonderful to see her smiling all the time.

The children have thrived at BYU-Idaho and Sugar-Salem High School, participating in many activities they never would have in Utah.

The biggest surprise so far is that our fourth child, Leah, met a wonderful man named Adam Murphy at a BYU-Idaho country dance, and they were married in the Rexburg Temple six months after she graduated from high school. That certainly wouldn't have happened if we hadn't moved! An added benefit is we can see the Grand Tetons from our yard, so life is good!

This is not an indication anyone else needs to pack up and head to Idaho. It just happens to be what our family needed to do at this time.

A Chosen Area

There's no denying, though, that the area we now live in is a special place. I recently made a business visit to Jackson, Wyoming. When the visit was done, I drove over the Teton Pass and down into Idaho. As I passed through Driggs and traveled west across the vast potato fields toward Rexburg, a shaft of light broke through the clouds and shined on the town of Ashton off in the distance.

The scene was strikingly beautiful and symbolic, because I've had many strong impressions of how the Upper Snake River Valley will someday soon be a great haven for the pure in heart who seek to follow the Savior.

As I peered across the valley, I sensed how it has been prepared by the Lord as a refuge from the coming storms. The people who are gathering there are humble servants of God who have heeded the promptings to prepare for the future.

As I drove along, the clouds moved away, and sunlight flooded the valley. My heart was nearly bursting with joy as a vision opened up to me that progressed like a futuristic time sequence. First I saw thousands of tents fill the valley in organized clusters a few miles apart. Then the tents were replaced by modest homes, and finally a magnificent City of Light emerged that will stand through the Millennium.

I realized the Lord is preparing many similar areas to be places of refuge from the coming tribulations. This joyful feeling accompanied me all the way home, reminding me that although the world is facing some dark times, a glorious reality soon awaits the faithful Saints.

Tammy and I at the Upper Mesa Falls overlook, about a half-hour from our new home.

Leah's wedding in January 2017 to Adam Murphy in the Rexburg Temple was a frigid but delightful day.

CHAPTER TWENTY-FOUR

❧

Looking to the Future

Soon after I had my second near-death experience in 1993, I was driving south along I-15 in Orem, Utah. I looked to the right and saw the dozens of buildings comprising Geneva Steel, where my dad worked.

Then the scene changed, similar to what had happened to me on the road near Manti when I saw a vision of tents in the wheat fields. I suddenly had an unobstructed view all the way to Utah Lake. Geneva Steel's smokestacks and large buildings were gone, and it looked like there were new subdivisions built on the land. I was told by the Spirit that this transformation would happen before any major natural disasters hit Utah County.

This actually came as a welcome vision, because I couldn't imagine that scene happening for several years, or even for a few decades. Geneva Steel was doing well at the time, and even if it did shut down, it would take a monumental effort to clear away all of the buildings and equipment.

That didn't include the challenge of removing all of the hazardous materials to make the area habitable again. I just couldn't see a private company, or even the federal government, spending the time and effort to do that.

Well, by the year 1999, Geneva Steel was struggling, and it

officially shut its doors in 2001. Within three years a deal was worked out for companies from China and India to buy most of the steel-making equipment. Other companies took care of the redevelopment of the land, and now homes and businesses are found there.

I prefer a calm, peaceful life and a safe society, but it is ominous to me that the land where Geneva Steel once stood now matches what I saw in that vision.

I don't know when an earthquake will come, but I have seen in vision the damage it will cause. I hope we still have a few years before it strikes, but it would be best to be prepared if it comes sooner. One certainty is that the Lord Jesus Christ is in charge. His prophet and apostles will guide the Saints and lead the righteous to safety at the proper time.

How My Novels Are Written

My novels are filled with many trials and triumphs that will occur among the Saints in the coming years. The most common question I receive is, "What parts of your books are based on what you've seen in vision, and what parts did you make up?"

The short answer is that I don't fictionalize any of the events portrayed. I'm really not that creative. Let me describe how my writing process occurs.

My torn veil allows information to be downloaded into my brain from the other side. The scenes I am shown are real events that will happen, but it is my job to fit them into the lives of the fictional families in my novels.

I always try to write my books in a priesthood-dedicated location that allows the Spirit to flow freely. Since moving to Idaho, the BYU-Idaho Library is my favorite place to write. There's a certain corner in the library where I can look out the window and see the BYU-Idaho Center.

When I'm able to write without interruption, I can write up to 10 pages in two or three hours. As I pray and focus on a particular chapter, scenes open up to me. I simply type into my laptop what I'm seeing. It is like watching a snippet of a movie, and once I get the details of that snippet typed in, another scene is placed in my mind.

When I see the scenes, I rarely hear the dialogue. So if any part is fabricated, that would be it. However, I do feel guided in what comes out of the characters' mouths, and I might spend three or four minutes rewriting a conversation until it feels right.

I Am Mark Dalton

I've mentioned before that my novels are based on what I have been shown regarding my children's future, but it is important to remember that the fictional Dalton family only has two children, Emma and Doug. The experiences the characters have are a combination of what I've seen regarding my five children.

In other words, my daughter Emma's life course isn't going to fully match her fictional counterpart, because so many other experiences have been merged in the novels with what I've seen regarding her siblings.

It is best this way. The kids have a general sense of what lies ahead for them, but they don't feel their future is predetermined. Rest assured that they rely on their patriarchal blessings for guidance, not their dad's novels.

However, putting two and two together, it means in my *Standing in Holy Places* series that fictional Emma's father Mark Dalton is loosely based on my own future.

I have seen myself in vision as an older man having the wonderful opportunity of helping build New Jerusalem. I appeared to be in better shape in the future than I am now, probably due to the lack of fast food restaurants in Zion.

I hope my novels show that wonderful days are coming for the Saints of God. Don't be paralyzed by fear. Just steadily prepare yourself both physically and spiritually. The coming trials can be compared to an intense thunderstorm that we will endure together. Then after the clouds pass, we'll bask in the glorious light of the Son of God.

A Glorious Reunion

As I pondered how to close this book, my mind was drawn to the wonderful people I have mentioned who are now on the other side of the veil. I thought of Keith, Rosalie, Guy, Flora, Lucille and many other ancestors are watching over me and my relatives.

I pictured myself standing in the center of the Springville Evergreen Cemetery. I saw people dressed in white emerging from all areas of the cemetery. I recognized a contingent of Daybell relatives coming toward me, led by Keith and Rosalie walking hand in hand.

Then from the east came my Chesnut grandparents from their burial sites. Guy and Flora glowed with purity and light as they approached. I hugged each one of them, and the love that radiated from them was overpowering.

I looked around and saw many other relatives gathering with us, including Tammy and our parents. The circle continued to grow as we put our arms around each other and cried tears of joy. I saw Lucille join Tammy and Phyllis. She gave them a big hug and said, "We did it!"

I realized that achieving salvation is a great team effort that is happening on both sides of the veil. When that glorious day arrives when we earn our reward, we will share it with those we love. I'm looking forward to it!

Novels by Chad Daybell

The Emma Trilogy
An Errand for Emma
Doug's Dilemma
Escape to Zion

Chasing Paradise (*a prequel to the novels below*)

The Standing in Holy Places Series
Book One: The Great Gathering
Book Two: The Celestial City
Book Three: The Rise of Zion
Book Four: The Keys of the Kingdom
Book Five: The Renewed Earth

The Times of Turmoil Series
Book One: Evading Babylon
Book Two: Martial Law
Book Three: Days of Fury
Book Four: Reclaiming Liberty (*coming soon*)

Other Non-fiction Titles
Baptism: Entering the Path to Eternal Life
Through the Eyes of John (*illustrated by Rhett Murray*)
The Aaronic Priesthood
The Tiny Talks Series: Volumes 1 through 4
One Foot in the Grave
The Youth of Zion